Death and the Afterlife

The Berkeley Tanner Lectures

The Tanner Lectures on Human Values were established by the American scholar, industrialist, and philanthropist Obert Clark Tanner; they are presented annually at nine universities in the United States and England. The University of California, Berkeley became a permanent host of annual Tanner Lectures in the academic year 2000–2001. This work is the eighth in a series of books based on the Berkeley Tanner Lectures. The volume includes a revised version of the two lectures that Samuel Scheffler gave at Berkeley in March of 2012, along with a third essay on a closely related theme. These are followed by comments by Susan Wolf, Harry G. Frankfurt, Seana Shiffrin, and Niko Kolodny, and a final rejoinder by Professor Scheffler. The volume is edited by Professor Kolodny, who also contributes an introduction. The Berkeley Tanner Lecture Series was established in the belief that these distinguished lectures, together with the lively debates stimulated by their presentation in Berkeley, deserve to be made available to a wider audience. Additional volumes are in preparation.

MARTIN JAY
R. JAY WALLACE
Series Editors

Volumes Published in the Series

JOSEPH RAZ, *The Practice of Value*
Edited by R. JAY WALLACE
With Christine M. Korsgard, Robert Pippin, and Bernard Williams

FRANK KERMODE, *Pleasure and Change: The Aesthetics of Canon*
Edited by ROBERT ALTER
With Geoffrey Hartman, John Guillory, and Carey Perloff

SEYLA BENHABIB, *Another Cosmopolitanism*
Edited by ROBERT POST
With Jeremy Waldron, Bonnie Honig, and Will Kymlicka

AXEL HONNETH, *Reification: A New Look at an Old Idea*
Edited by MARTIN JAY
With Judith Butler, Raymond Geuss, and Jonathan Lear

ALLAN GIBBARD, *Reconciling Our Aims*
Edited by BARRY STROUD
With Michael Bratman, John Broome, and F. M. Kamm

DEREK PARFIT, *On What Matters: Volumes 1 & 2*
Edited by SAMUEL SCHEFFLER
With T. M. Scanlon, Susan Wolf, Allen Wood, and Barbara Herman

JEREMY WALDRON, *Dignity, Rank, and Rights*
Edited by MEIR DAN-COHEN
With Wai Chee Dimock, Don Herzog, and Michael Rosen

Death and the Afterlife

SAMUEL SCHEFFLER

With Commentaries by
SUSAN WOLF
HARRY G. FRANKFURT
SEANA VALENTINE SHIFFRIN
NIKO KOLODNY

Edited and Introduced by
NIKO KOLODNY

OXFORD
UNIVERSITY PRESS

Oxford University Press is a department of the
University of Oxford. It furthers the University's objective
of excellence in research, scholarship, and education
by publishing worldwide.

Oxford   New York
Auckland   Cape Town   Dar es Salaam   Hong Kong   Karachi
Kuala Lumpur   Madrid   Melbourne   Mexico City   Nairobi
New Delhi   Shanghai   Taipei   Toronto

With offices in
Argentina   Austria   Brazil   Chile   Czech Republic   France   Greece
Guatemala   Hungary   Italy   Japan   Poland   Portugal   Singapore
South Korea   Switzerland   Thailand   Turkey   Ukraine   Vietnam

Oxford is a registered trademark of Oxford University
Press in the UK and certain other countries.

Published in the United States of America by
Oxford University Press
198 Madison Avenue, New York, NY 10016

Library of Congress Cataloging-in-Publication Data
Scheffler, Samuel, 1951–
Death and the afterlife / Samuel Scheffler ; with commentaries by
Harry Frankfurt, Niko Kolodny, Seana Shiffrin, Susan Wolf;
edited and introduced by Niko Kolodny.
pages cm.—(The Berkeley Tanner lectures)
Includes index.
ISBN 978-0-19-998250-9 (alk. paper)
1. Life.   2. Egoism.   3. Values.
4. Motivation (Psychology).   I. Kolodny, Niko.   II. Title.
BD435.S29   2013   128'.5—dc23   2013001134

1 3 5 7 9 8 6 4 2
Printed in the United States of America
on acid-free paper

Contents

DEATH AND THE AFTERLIFE

SAMUEL SCHEFFLER

COMMENTS

REPLY TO COMMENTATORS

SAMUEL SCHEFFLER

Acknowledgments

The first two lectures included in this volume, which together have the title "The Afterlife," were presented as the Tanner Lectures on Human Values at the University of California at Berkeley in March 2012. I am deeply grateful to the Berkeley Tanner Lectures Committee for inviting me to deliver the lectures and to the Tanner Foundation for its generous sponsorship.

While I was preparing the lectures for delivery at Berkeley, I benefited from the opportunity to present versions of the lecture material in a number of different settings, including a conference at the University of Iceland; Philosophy Department colloquia at Harvard and UCLA; the Colloquium on Legal, Political, and Social Philosophy at NYU Law School; the Colloquium in Legal and Social Philosophy at University College London; and my graduate seminar at NYU in the fall of 2010. A version was also presented as the 2011 John Passmore Lecture at the Australian National University. I am grateful to the members of those audiences, as well as the audience at Berkeley, for valuable discussion that led to many improvements. I am conscious of specific debts to Selim Berker, Eugene Chislenko, Ronald Dworkin, Samuel Freeman, Pamela Hieronymi, Dale Jamieson, Hyunseop Kim, Christine Korsgaard, Liam Murphy, Thomas Nagel, Derek Parfit, Philip Pettit, Adam Scheffler, Michael Smith, and David Wiggins. And I am particularly grateful to Monika Betzler, Agnes Callard, Ruth Chang, Hannah Ginsborg, Stephen Guest, János Kis, Orsolya Reich, John Tasioulas, and Katja Vogt, each of whom provided me with instructive written comments.

The third lecture ("Fear, Death, and Confidence") was originally written for a conference about the legacy of Bernard Williams's work that was held at the University of Chicago in October 2011. It develops naturally out of the first two lectures, and the entire set of three lectures is meant to constitute a unified whole. I thank Jonathan Lear, the organizer of the Chicago conference, for inviting me to participate. Versions of the third lecture were also presented to Philosophy Department colloquia at CUNY, Union College, Ohio University, Rutgers University, the University of Bern, and the University of Pennsylvania. I am indebted to all those audiences for their questions and objections, and to Agnes Callard, Jonathan Lear, Matthew Lister, Katja Vogt, and Mark Wunderlich for helpful written comments.

My debts to the four commentators whose contributions are included in this volume—Harry Frankfurt, Niko Kolodny, Seana Shiffrin, and Susan Wolf—are substantial, and I very much appreciate the time and attention they have devoted to my work. In my concluding responses I have tried, no doubt with limited success, to address the many significant issues they have raised.

Finally, I must express special thanks to Niko Kolodny, who, in addition to contributing a formal commentary to the volume, gave me informal written comments on earlier drafts of all three lectures and the concluding responses. He has also been an ideal volume editor, and the book has benefited enormously from his efficiency, conscientiousness, and good judgment.

Samuel Scheffler
December 2012

Contributors

SAMUEL SCHEFFLER is University Professor in the Department of Philosophy at New York University. He works primarily in the areas of moral and political philosophy and the theory of value. His books and articles have addressed central questions in ethical theory, and he has also written on topics as diverse as equality, nationalism and cosmopolitanism, toleration, terrorism, immigration, tradition, and the moral significance of personal relationships. He is author of *Equality and Tradition* (2010), *Boundaries and Allegiances* (2001), *Human Morality* (1992), and *The Rejection of Consequentialism* (1982).

HARRY G. FRANKFURT is Professor Emeritus at Princeton University. His books include the bestseller *On Bullshit* (2005) and *Taking Ourselves Seriously and Getting It Right* (2006), which is based on his Tanner Lectures at Stanford University in 2004. He is also author of *On Truth* (2006), *The Reasons of Love* (2004), *Necessity, Volition, and Love* (1999), *The Importance of What We Care About* (1988), and *Demons, Dreamers, and Madmen* (1970).

NIKO KOLODNY is Professor of Philosophy at the University of California, Berkeley. He works in moral and political philosophy, and has written papers on love, rationality, and promises, among other subjects.

SEANA VALENTINE SHIFFRIN is Professor of Philosophy and Pete Kameron Professor of Law and Social Justice at the University of California, Los Angeles. She has published many articles on a wide range of topics, including the demands of morality, the ethics of procreation, freedom of speech, promising, contracts, torts, and intellectual property. She will deliver the Tanner Lectures at Berkeley in 2017.

SUSAN WOLF is Edna J. Koury Professor of Philosophy at the University of North Carolina, Chapel Hill. Her books include *Understanding Love: Philosophy, Film, and Fiction* (2013), an anthology of essays co-edited with Christopher Grau; *Meaning in Life and Why It Matters* (2010), which is based on her Tanner Lectures at Princeton University in 2007; and *Freedom Within Reason* (1990).

Death and the Afterlife

Introduction

Niko Kolodny

A line attributed to Woody Allen goes: "I don't want to achieve immortality through my work, I want to achieve immortality through not dying. I don't want to live on in the hearts of my countrymen, I want to live on in my apartment."[1] Part of the joke's effect comes from the abrupt drop from lofty metaphor (living on in hearts) to pedestrian literalness (living on in apartments). Part just comes from Allen's nebbishy, self-deprecating persona. (Leave world-historical fame and noble self-sacrifice to others; a prewar walk-up is enough for me.) What strikes a more sustained chord, though, is the joke's bleak knowingness, a kind typical of gallows humor. Try as you might to console or distract yourselves with substitutes, what matters—and deep down we all know this—is simply not dying.

In the papers that form the core of this book, Samuel Scheffler suggests that, while our situation may not be more reassuring, it is at least more complicated. What happens *after* we die may be more important *to* us, and our *not* dying may be less important *for* us, than Allen's joke, or the sentiment it resonates with, would have it. This is not because Scheffler aims to show that we will somehow survive our deaths or should be unusually selfless. He makes his case simply by asking us to reflect carefully on what we do value and what our valuing it requires.

1. The first sentence appears in Linda Sunshine, ed., *The Illustrated Woody Allen Reader* (New York: Alfred A. Knopf, 1993), 250. Although I have not been able to find an authoritative source for the second sentence, I'm not alone in remembering it and attributing it to Allen. See http://en.wikiquote.org/wiki/Immortality.

Set aside for a moment the prospect of living on in the hearts of your countrymen, or achieving immortality through your work, and simply focus on the more basic expectation that this prospect presupposes: that people will live after you die. Without this "collective afterlife," Scheffler argues, it is not clear that your life could be filled with the values that it is. This includes some of the pedestrian values (e.g., take-out Chinese, the Yankees on WPIX) that you might enjoy in your apartment right now, values that have little, if anything, to do with grander hopes of you "living on" in the memory of others. Granted, we may be disappointed if we look to the collective afterlife for stand-ins or consolation prizes for personal immortality. But we shouldn't overlook how the collective afterlife supports the meaning of our finite, mortal lives here and now. On the other hand, Scheffler suggests, as natural as it is to want to live on in your apartment, this want makes little sense. Perhaps you might stay in your apartment and never die. That seems conceptually, if not biologically, possible. But this would not be a continuation of the life that you want, or even of anything you could recognize as a life at all. For your life depends not only for its value, but also for its very shape and definition, on the fact that it will come to an end.

Scheffler presented the two parts of "The Afterlife" as the Tanner Lectures on Human Values at the University of California, Berkeley, in March of 2012. The campus was fortunate on that occasion to have comments by three distinguished philosophers: Susan Wolf, Harry Frankfurt, and Seana Shiffrin. This book contains the full text of Scheffler's Tanner Lectures, only slightly revised, along with a third lecture, which was shared with the commentators after the event, "Fear, Death, and Confidence." These are followed by commentaries by Wolf, Frankfurt, and Shiffrin, which are based on the remarks they gave at Berkeley, and so engage primarily with "The Afterlife." There is also a fourth commentary, by the editor and author of this introduction, which mostly addresses "Fear, Death, and Confidence." The volume concludes with Scheffler's response to the commentaries, which, in addition to replying to specific objections, expands on the broader ideas of the lectures in an exploratory spirit.[2]

The "afterlife" of Scheffler's title is not the personal "life after death" posited by so many religious and mystical traditions, but instead the "collective afterlife" described above: the existence of other human beings after our death. What role in our lives, he asks, is played by our assumption that there will be such a collective afterlife? It would be natural to expect an introduction to these lectures to explain their relation to earlier treatments of the same question. But part of what makes his question so stimulating is that it is not clear that any philosopher has asked it before. As Frankfurt observes in his commentary, it is "pretty much original with [Scheffler] ... [H]e has effectively opened up a new and promising field of philosophical inquiry. Not bad going, in a discipline to which many of the very best minds have already devoted themselves for close to three thousand years."

Partly because he is raising new questions, Scheffler does not proceed by building on, or criticizing, established principles. Instead, as the most evocative philosophy often does, his lectures invite us to conduct a series of thought experiments and then to try to come to terms with our reactions to them. In the "doomsday scenario," everyone dies thirty days after your death. In the "infertility scenario," suggested to Scheffler by P. D. James's novel, *The Children of Men* (made into a movie of the same name in 2006 by Alfonso Cuarón), no babies are born.[3] It is hard not to find these scenarios, as Scheffler finds them, unsettling. But why? In the doomsday scenario, you don't die prematurely. And in the infertility scenario, no one at all dies prematurely. Everyone now alive lives on as long, if not as fully, as she otherwise would. What is unsettling,

2. The preparation of the manuscript for publication benefitted greatly from the work of Eugene Chislenko.

3. P. D. James, *The Children of Men* (London: Faber and Faber, 1992).

then, is just the end of humanity itself, the not-coming-to-be of mere strangers.

Scheffler's "afterlife conjecture" speaks to how deeply and pervasively unsettling this might be. If we were to learn that there was no afterlife, if we were to find ourselves in the doomsday or infertility scenario, the conjecture says, a wide range of things that now matter to us would no longer do so. We would no longer value them, where "valuing" involves cognitive, motivational, and affective elements. We would lose confidence in the belief in their value, we would see ourselves as having weaker reasons to engage with them, and we would become emotionally deadened to them, as if by depression or ennui.

What pursuits might come to matter to us less? The examples that seem least controversial and easiest to explain involve objectives that won't be achieved, or won't benefit anyone, if there is no afterlife. Would we feel driven to spend our days in the lab developing biofuels or commercial fusion, when no one will be around to finish what we started, let alone enjoy its fruits? It also doesn't take much imagination to worry that our investment in pursuits that belong to larger collaborative enterprises, extended over time, might be similarly undermined, even though they do not aim at any specific, datable payoff. This would seem to include contributions to art, literature, and knowledge, as well as participation in cultural, religious, and institutional traditions. And in James's imagining, which has a ring of truth, the disappearance of the afterlife somehow hollows out a wide range of forms of appreciation and enjoyment, including even simple pleasures, like a good meal. Perhaps, in the face of the doomsday or infertility scenarios we would still want to avoid pain, bodily deprivation, and psychic distress. But how much more would matter to us, Scheffler observes, is not at all clear.

In their challenging and probing commentaries, Wolf and Frankfurt make cases for the resilience of value without the afterlife. Why should, say, the appreciation of music, or the satisfaction of completing a painting, or the solace that we might find in comforting others here and now depend on our expecting humanity to have a future? Note that while these questions may be asked by those who are less convinced than Scheffler *that* the afterlife conjecture is true, they might also be asked, less rhetorically, by those who simply want to understand better *why* the conjecture is true. Scheffler offers several speculative, but highly suggestive, answers. Perhaps the absence of the afterlife would put even simple pleasures out of reach, for example, because these goods have a place only within a "human life as a whole," and "our conception of 'a human life as a whole' relies on an implicit understanding of such a life as itself occupying a place in an ongoing human history." In her constructive and imaginative commentary, Shiffrin sheds further light on this question, approaching it from a somewhat different angle. The mere loss of what we value, she observes, is not so distressing in itself; old forms pass away all the time to be replaced by new ones. Perhaps what is particularly distressing about the doomsday and infertility scenarios, then, has to do with the *arbitrariness* of the loss of what we value: that art, literature, scholarship, and so on, would end *for no good reason*.

In any event, Scheffler doesn't aim to have the final word, especially in an inquiry that, if Frankfurt is right, has only just gotten under way. What he does stress, and this seems surely right, is the need to proceed with care. The values that we know of have been experienced only against a more or less settled, unreflective expectation of the afterlife. We cannot assume that they would survive in its absence, particularly given the intuitive power of the doomsday and infertility scenarios.

The afterlife conjecture might be paired with what could be called the "immortality conjecture": that if we were to learn that we and everyone we knew were not immortal, then our lives would be similarly blighted. Here, of course, no thought experiment is needed. We have actually conducted the experiment, and its result is resoundingly negative. Despite knowing that we and everyone we know will die, we carry on more or less confident and invested in our pursuits. This throws into relief a surprising, indeed astonishing, contrast. In some sense, the collective afterlife—the existence of people unknown to us and, indeed, as yet unborn—actually matters more to us than the continued existence of ourselves or anyone else now alive. As Scheffler puts it, "the coming into existence of people we do not know and love matters more to us than our own survival and the survival of the people we do know and love."

Yet, someone might reply, just as the immortality conjecture has already been put to the test, hasn't the afterlife conjecture already been put to the test? And isn't the result just as resoundingly negative? After all, we know that humanity will *eventually* come to an end, if only millennia from now, and yet it strikes us as absurd to respond to this knowledge by packing it in today. In this, Wolf sees a possible rational basis for confidence even in the face of the doomsday or infertility scenario. If equanimity is the correct response to the certain, eventual disappearance of the afterlife, she suggests, then why not revise our initial dismay about its imagined, imminent disappearance? Scheffler observes, however, that this is just one way of resolving the tension between our responses to the eventual and imminent end of mankind. Other, less comforting, resolutions seem no less reasonable.

If the afterlife conjecture is correct, Scheffler observes, then it complicates, in subtle but far-reaching ways, prevalent assumptions about human individualism and egoism. It suggests limits to our individualism, in that it reveals that much of what we value, even if not overtly social, depends on implicit collective preconditions. And it suggests limits to our egoism, in that it reveals that we are more emotionally vulnerable to what happens to other people, even people as distant from us as other human beings can be. All the comments (save Shiffrin's) express one or another reservation about the suggestion that the afterlife conjecture shows us to be any less egoistic. As with many philosophical debates, however, the controversy seems dispelled as soon as its terms are clearly defined. Scheffler's point, again, is that the afterlife conjecture reveals that we are more *emotionally* dependent on what happens to others than we might have thought. This does not necessarily mean that we are less "egoistic" in the sense of being more *motivated* to care for others. Nor need it mean that the emotional dependence on others that the afterlife conjecture reveals is not, in a way, "self-interested"; too crudely put, we need others to live so that our *own* lives can have value. Perhaps the lesson to draw is that the afterlife conjecture reveals not only the limits of our egoism, in Scheffler's stipulated sense, but also the limits of our *vocabulary* of "egoism." Our engagement with the fates of others is more complex and varied than "egoism," with its traditional opposition to altruism, is likely to capture.

"Fear, Death, and Confidence" turns our attention away from our attitudes about the future of humanity toward more familiar (or more familiarly discussed) attitudes about our own personal mortality. What attitude, Scheffler asks, is it reasonable to have toward one's own death? Here too Scheffler finds our outlook on our mortality arrestingly paradoxical. In a sense, we need to die in order to live; our life must have an end for it to be a meaningful life, or indeed a life at all. For all that, however, our fear of death is not unreasonable.

The suggestion that immortality might deprive our lives of meaning is not entirely new. Bernard Williams, to take perhaps the best-known example, argues for something like this in his essay, "The Makropulos Case."[4] For Williams, however, the idea often seems to be that a life that went on *too long* would eventually *lose* its meaning. Death, provided it comes soon enough, is what rescues us from that fate. Scheffler's point is more fundamental. A life lived

---

4. Bernard Williams, "The Makropulos Case: Reflections on the Tedium of Immortality," in *Problems of the Self* (Cambridge: Cambridge University Press, 1973), 82–100.

beyond the shadow of death would not be, even "early on," a meaningful life, or even a life at all.

Why? In part, because our conception of a life is a conception of a progression through a finite number of stages—childhood, adolescence, old age—of more or less fixed duration. In part, because many values are, or involve, forms of protection or relief from disvalues such as disease, harm, and danger, which themselves depend on the prospect of death. And in part, perhaps most importantly, because valuing things, with its comparative and prioritizing judgments, makes sense only against a background of scarcity, and, in particular, temporal scarcity.

It might be suggested that some of these features could be present, to some extent, even if the prospect of death were absent. Perhaps, for instance, there would still be the danger of pain or humiliation, if not loss of life. But it is hard even to know how to evaluate this suggestion, given how pervasively the fact of our mortality structures our thinking about life and the goods it might contain. As in his reply to Wolf's and Frankfurt's comparative optimism about value without the afterlife, Scheffler cautions against our assuming too easily that we can continue to make sense of value once it has been torn from the only contexts in which we have had any experience of it.

If Scheffler is right, then to want eternal life, or never to die, is confused. A life that goes on forever is not possible, and never dying would be a disaster for us, precisely because it would deny us a life. All the same, recognition of this fact may do little to palliate our fear of death. And Scheffler sees no clear reason why it should. Indeed, he suggests, even though we need to die in order to live, our fear of death may have deeper and more tenacious roots than many philosophical traditions recognize. I may fear my death not only because it deprives me of certain identifiable future goods, such as seeing my children grow up. I may fear my death, and not unreasonably, also simply because of what my death is: the ceasing to exist of the very subject of this fear.

The most striking of Scheffler's conclusions may be the contrast that finally emerges when the findings of "The Afterlife"—about our attitudes toward others' survival—are placed against the findings of "Fear, Death, and Confidence"—about our attitudes toward our own survival. Whereas the expectation that others will survive me, that humanity will go on, is necessary for my valuing much of what I do, the recognition that I will *not* survive, that my life will *not* go on, is likewise necessary for my valuing much of what I do. What I need, as he puts it, is that I "should die and that others should live." In the most abstract terms, one might say, our conception of a valuable life makes seemingly incompatible demands. It needs both an end and continuation. It needs to be bounded by temporal limits but also to partake, somehow, of ongoing enterprise. What makes this paradoxical combination, and so value itself, possible for us, is that we are at once mortal and social. My own death bends my life into a significant arc, but that arc is traced against a collective history that carries on.

This conclusion may not be consoling, exactly, and it is not, I take it, Scheffler's expectation that it will be. Indeed, as he notes, it may just as soon disconcert us, by bringing to light vulnerabilities and conflicting impulses that we did not know we had. Instead, the hope is that pursuing such questions will bring us to a better understanding of our complex and elusive attitudes toward our own and others' survival. It is a hope that is amply fulfilled by Scheffler's reflections and the discussion that they have only just begun to provoke.

Death and the Afterlife

SAMUEL SCHEFFLER

Lecture 1: The Afterlife (Part I)

1.

My title is, I confess, a bit of a tease. Like many people nowadays, though unlike many others, I do not believe in the existence of an afterlife as normally understood. That is, I do not believe that individuals continue to live on as conscious beings after their biological deaths. To the contrary, I believe that biological death represents the final and irrevocable end of an individual's life. So one thing I will not be doing in these lectures is arguing for the existence of the afterlife as it is commonly understood. At the same time, however, I take it for granted that other human beings will continue to live on after my own death. To be sure, I am aware that human life on earth could, via a number of different routes, come to a sudden and catastrophic end at any time, and that it will, in any case, come to an end eventually. Still, I normally take it for granted that life will go on long after I myself am gone, and in this rather nonstandard sense, I take it for granted that there will be an afterlife: that others will continue to live after I have died. I believe that most of us take this for granted, and it is one of the aims of these lectures to investigate the role of this assumption in our lives.

It is my contention that the existence of an afterlife, in my nonstandard sense of "afterlife," matters greatly to us. It matters to us in its own right, and it matters to us because our confidence in the existence of an afterlife is a condition of many other things that we care about continuing to matter to us. Or so I shall try to show. If my contention is correct, it reveals some surprising features of our attitudes toward our own deaths. In addition, I will argue that the importance to us of the afterlife can help to illuminate what, more generally, is involved in something's *mattering* or *being important* to us, or in our *valuing* it. Finally, the role of the afterlife sheds light on the profound but elusive influence of time in our thinking about ourselves, and it affords a convenient point of entry for investigating the various strategies we use for coming to terms with the temporal dimension of our lives.

Most of the attitudes I will discuss, both toward the afterlife and toward what happens during our lives, are in one sense very familiar, almost embarrassingly so. There is very little that I will be saying in these lectures that we don't, on some level, already know. Nevertheless, I believe that the attitudes I will discuss can bear additional scrutiny. As I have tried to suggest, I think that we can learn something about ourselves by reflecting on them, and some of what we learn may even surprise us.

As I have already indicated, the attitudes I have in mind involve a family of related concepts, such as the concept of *valuing* a thing, or *caring* about it, or of the thing's *mattering* or *being important* to us. Each of these concepts differs in some respects from the others, and the differences are significant for some purposes. Elsewhere, I have examined the concept of valuing in particular, and I want to begin by saying something about how I understand that notion.[1] Like many others who have written on the topic, I believe that there is an important distinction between valuing something and believing that it is valuable. Valuing, in my view, comprises a complex syndrome of interrelated attitudes and dispositions, which includes but is not limited to a belief that the valued item is valuable. Valuing something normally involves, in addition to such a belief, at least the following elements: a susceptibility to experience a range of context-dependent emotions concerning the valued item, a

---

1. "Valuing," in *Equality and Tradition* (New York: Oxford University Press, 2010), ch. 1, 15–40.

disposition to experience those emotions as being merited or deserved, and a disposition to treat certain kinds of considerations pertaining to the valued item as reasons for action in relevant deliberative contexts. Thus, valuing is an attitudinal phenomenon that has doxastic, deliberative, motivational, and emotional dimensions.

As I have said, the other concepts I have mentioned—the concept of *caring* about something or of the thing's *mattering* or *being important* to us—differ from the concept of valuing, and from each other, in ways that deserve attention, but I will not provide that attention here. For the purposes of this discussion, what these concepts have in common is more important than the ways in which they differ. Or so, at any rate, I will assume. I will rely from time to time on the account of valuing that I have just sketched, but I will also draw freely on other members of this family of concepts as the context seems to me to demand, and I will not investigate the relations among them nor will I comment explicitly on the ways in which they differ from one another.

I have said that I want to investigate certain of *our* attitudes, and so let me say a word about how I am using the first-person plural pronoun. When I talk about *our* attitudes and what *we* think or feel, I do not intend to be making strictly universal claims. I do not mean to claim, in other words, that literally everyone is prone to these attitudes. My use of the first-person plural might instead be thought of, to borrow some terminology that David Lewis employed in a related context, as a "wait-and-see" use. In explaining his version of a dispositional theory of value, Lewis wrote:

> In making a judgment of value, one makes many claims at once, some stronger than others, some less confidently than others, and waits to see which can be made to stick. I say X is a value; I mean that all mankind are disposed to value X; or anyway all nowadays are; or anyway all nowadays are except maybe some peculiar people on distant islands; or anyway ...; or anyway you and I, talking here and now, are; or anyway I am. How much am I claiming?— as much as I can get away with. If my stronger claims were proven

false...I still mean to stand by the weaker ones. So long as I'm not challenged, there's no need to back down in advance; and there's no need to decide how far I'd back down if pressed.[2]

To put it a slightly different way, in characterizing *our* attitudes, I mean to be characterizing my own attitudes and the attitudes of any other people who share them, however numerous those people happen to be. On the one hand, I don't think that the attitudes are mine alone. On the other hand, I don't wish to claim that they are universally shared, and so in that respect I am prepared to be more concessive from the outset than is Lewis. Indeed, one limitation on the scope of my claims was implicit in my opening remarks. The attitudes I will describe are, in the first instance, the attitudes of people who, like me, do not believe in the afterlife as traditionally understood. What my discussion reveals about the attitudes of those who do believe in the traditional afterlife is a topic to which I will return briefly at the end of the second lecture. In the meantime, my discussion of "our" attitudes will proceed on the assumption that "we" do not believe that we will live on after our own deaths. Despite this limitation, I believe that the attitudes I will describe are common enough to be of interest.

2.

I will begin by asking you to consider a crude and morbid thought experiment. Suppose you knew that, although you yourself would live a normal life span, the earth would be completely destroyed thirty days after your death in a collision with a giant asteroid. How would this knowledge affect your attitudes during the remainder of your life? Now, rather than respond straightaway,

---

2. David Lewis, "Dispositional Theories of Value," in *Papers in Ethics and Social Philosophy* (Cambridge: Cambridge University Press, 2000), 68–94, at 85.

you may well protest that I haven't given you enough information to go on. How, in my imagined scenario, are we to suppose that you acquired your doomsday knowledge? Are other people in on the secret, or is this devastating piece of information your solitary burden to bear? I haven't told you, and yet surely the answers to these questions might affect your reactions. I freely concede these points. I also concede that, even if I were to fill in the story in the greatest possible detail, I would still be asking you to make conjectures about your attitudes under what I trust are highly counterfactual circumstances. Such conjectures, you may point out, are of questionable reliability and in any case impossible to verify. All this is true. But indulge me for a few minutes. Perhaps, despite the skimpiness of the description I have provided and the conjectural character of any response you may give, some things will seem relatively clear.

You won't be surprised to learn that, although I have asked you how you would react, I'm not going to let you speak for yourself, at least not just yet. Instead I'm going to make some conjectures of my own, conjectures about the kinds of reactions that you and I and others—that "we"—would be likely to have in the situation I have described. I will begin with a negative suggestion. One reaction that I think few of us would be likely to have, if confronted with my doomsday scenario, is complete indifference. For example, few of us would be likely to say, if told that the earth would be destroyed thirty days after our death: "So what? Since it won't happen until thirty days after my death, and since it won't hasten my death, it isn't of any importance to me. I won't be around to experience it, and so it doesn't matter to me in the slightest." The fact that we would probably not respond this way is already suggestive. It means that, at a minimum, we are not indifferent to everything that happens after our deaths. Something that will not happen until after our deaths can still matter or be important to us. And this in turn implies that things other than our own experiences matter to us. A postmortem event that matters to us would not be one of our experiences.

As against this, someone might object that, although the post-mortem event would not be one of our experiences, our prospective contemplation of that event would be part of our experience, and if such contemplation distressed us, then that distress too would be part of our experience. This is undeniable, but it is also beside the point. It does not show that only our own experiences matter to us. In the case at hand, what would matter to us, in the first instance, would not be our distress—though that might matter to us too—but rather the predicted postmortem event whose contemplation gave rise to that distress. If the postmortem event did not matter to us, there would be nothing for us to be distressed about in the first place. So, as I have said, the fact that we would not react to the doomsday scenario with indifference suggests that things that happen after our deaths sometimes matter to us, and that in turn implies that things other than our own experiences matter to us. In this sense, the fact that we would not react with indifference supports a *nonexperientialist* interpretation of our values. It supports an interpretation according to which it is not only our experiences that we value or that matter to us.[3]

There is another reaction to the doomsday scenario that I think few of us would be likely to have. Few of us, I think, would be likely to deliberate about the good and bad consequences of the destruction of the earth in order to decide whether it would, on balance, be a good or a bad thing. This is not, I think, because the answer is so immediately and overwhelmingly obvious that we don't need to perform the calculations. It is true, of course, that the destruction of the earth would have many horrible consequences. It would, for example, mean the end of all human joy, creativity, love, friendship, virtue, and happiness. So there are, undeniably, some weighty considerations to place in the minus column. On the other hand, it

3. To that extent, it supports the conclusions drawn by Robert Nozick in his discussion of "the experience machine" in *Anarchy, State, and Utopia* (New York: Basic Books, 1974), 42–45.

would also mean the end of all human suffering, cruelty, and injustice. No more genocide, no more torture, no more oppression, no more misery, no more pain. Surely these things all go in the plus column. And it's at least not *instantly* obvious that the minuses outweigh the pluses. Yet few of us, I think, would react to the scenario by trying to do the sums, by trying to figure out whether on balance the prospect of the destruction of the earth was welcome or unwelcome. On the face of it, at least, the fact that we would not react this way suggests that there is a *nonconsequentialist* dimension to our attitudes about what we value or what matters to us. It appears that what we value, or what matters to us, is not simply or solely that the best consequences, whatever they may be, should come to pass.[4]

Let us now move from negative to positive characterizations of our reactions. To begin with, I think it is safe to say that most of us would respond to the doomsday scenario with what I will generically call, with bland understatement, profound dismay. This is meant only as a superficial, placeholder characterization, which undoubtedly subsumes a range of more specific reactions. Many of these reactions have to do with the deaths of the particular people we love and the disappearance or destruction of the particular things that we care most about, where "things" is understood in a broad sense that encompasses not only physical objects but also social forms such as institutions, practices, activities, and ways of life. During our lifetimes,

---

4. Of course, someone might argue that, despite the appearances, our reactions do admit of a consequentialist interpretation. Perhaps, in reacting as we do, we simply jump to a possibly erroneous but nevertheless consequentialist conclusion, namely, that the negative consequences I have mentioned would outweigh the positive ones. Or perhaps we accept some axiology according to which the impersonal value of human existence per se is so great that any outcome in which human life continues is better than every outcome in which it does not. I don't find these claims very plausible, but I won't argue against them. One aim of these lectures is to offer a different account of why the continuation of human life matters so much to us.

we respond with grief, sadness, and other forms of distress to the sudden death of people we love and the sudden loss or destruction of things that we value deeply. We are bound to have similar reactions to the prospect that every particular person and thing that we treasure will soon be suddenly destroyed at once.

The fact that we would have these reactions highlights a *conservative* dimension in our attitudes toward what we value, which sits alongside the nonexperiential and nonconsequentialist dimensions already mentioned. In general, we want the people and things we care about to flourish; we are not indifferent to the destruction of that which matters most to us. Indeed, there is something approaching a conceptual connection between valuing something and wanting it to be sustained or preserved. During our lifetimes, this translates into a similarly close connection between valuing something and seeing reasons to act so as to preserve or sustain it ourselves. Part of the poignancy of contemplating our own deaths, under ordinary rather than doomsday conditions, is the recognition that we will no longer be able to respond to these reasons; we will not ourselves be able to help preserve or sustain the things that matter to us. We can, of course, take steps while we are alive to try to bring it about that other people will act after our deaths to preserve or sustain those things. For example, the devices of wills and bequests are important to us largely because they offer us—or seem to offer us—an opportunity to extend the reach of our own agency beyond death in an effort to help sustain the people and things that matter to us. In addition, some of the most elaborate and ingenious measures we take to try to ensure the postmortem preservation of our values are those we take as groups rather than as individuals, and I will discuss them at greater length later. But apart from taking steps now to influence the actions of others in the future, all we can really do is hope that the things that matter most to us will somehow be preserved or sustained. The doomsday scenario dashes all such hopes, and the emotional consequences of this, for someone facing this scenario, are likely to be profound.

In addition to the generic conservatism about value just noted, something more specific is involved in our reaction to the prospective destruction of the particular *people* we love and treasure. It is a feature of the scenario that I have described that all of our loved ones who survive thirty days beyond our own death will themselves die suddenly, violently, and prematurely, and this prospect itself is sufficient to fill us with horror and dread. In other words, it would fill us with horror and dread even if it were *only* our own loved ones who would be destroyed, and everything and everyone else would survive. Indeed, this dimension of our reaction is liable to be so powerful that it may make it difficult to notice some of the others. For this reason, I want to postpone discussion of it for a few minutes and to concentrate for a bit longer on our more general reactions to the doomsday scenario.

3.

I have so far said only that the prospect of the earth's imminent destruction would induce in us reactions of grief, sadness, and distress. But we must also consider how, if at all, it would affect our subsequent motivations and our choices about how to live. To what extent would we remain committed to our current projects and plans? To what extent would the activities in which we now engage continue to seem worth pursuing? Offhand, it seems that there are many projects and activities that might become less important to us. By this I mean several things. First, our reasons to engage in them might no longer seem to us as strong. At the limit, we might cease to see any reason to engage in them. Second, our emotional investment in them might weaken. For example, we might no longer feel as eager or excited at the prospect of engaging in them; as frustrated if prevented from engaging in them; as pleased if they seemed to be going well; as disappointed if they seemed not to be going well; and so on. At the limit, we might become emotionally detached from or indifferent to them. Third, our belief that they were worthwhile activities in which to engage might weaken or, at the limit, disappear altogether.

It is difficult to be sure exactly which projects and activities would seem to us diminished in importance in these respects, and no doubt there are interesting differences in the ways that different individuals would react. On the face of it, however, there are several types of projects and activities that would appear fairly obviously to be vulnerable to such changes in our attitudes. Consider, to take one representative example, the project of trying to find a cure for cancer. This project would seem vulnerable for at least two reasons. First, it is a project in which it is understood that ultimate success may be a long way off. Even the very best research that is done today may be but a step on a long road that will lead to a cure only in the indeterminate future, if at all. The doomsday scenario, by cutting the future short, makes it much less likely that such a cure will ever be found. Second, the primary value of the project lies in the prospect of eventually being able to cure the disease and to prevent the death and suffering it causes. But the doomsday scenario means that even immediate success in finding a cure would make available such benefits only for a very short period of time. Under these conditions, scientists' motivations to engage in such research might well weaken substantially. This suggests that projects would be specially vulnerable if either (a) their ultimate success is seen as something that may not be achieved until some time well in the future, or (b) the value of the project derives from the benefits that it will provide to large numbers of people over a long period of time. Cancer research is threatened because it satisfies both of these conditions. But there are many other projects and activities that satisfy at least one of them. This is true, for example, of much research in science, technology, and medicine. It is also true of much social and political activism. It is true of many efforts to build or reform or improve social institutions. It is true of many projects to build new buildings, improve the physical infrastructure of society, or protect the environment. No doubt you will be able to supply many other examples of your own.

The effect of the doomsday scenario on other types of projects is less clear. For example, many creative and scholarly projects have no obvious practical aim, such as finding a cure for cancer, but they are nevertheless undertaken with an actual or imagined audience or readership of some kind in mind. Although the doomsday scenario would not mean that audiences would disappear immediately, it would mean that they would not be around for very long. Would artistic, musical, and literary projects still seem worth undertaking? Would humanistic scholars continue to be motivated to engage in basic research? Would historians and theoretical physicists and anthropologists all carry on as before? Perhaps, but the answer is not obvious.

Nor is it merely projects of the kinds I have been discussing, as opposed to more routine aspects of human life, whose appeal might weaken or disappear. Consider, for example, procreative activity. Would people still be as motivated to have children if they knew that those children would die no later than thirty days after their own death? It seems unlikely that they would. But if they would not, then neither would they be as motivated to engage in the wide, varied, and life-altering array of activities associated with raising and caring for children. By contrast, the projects and activities that would seem least likely to be affected by the doomsday scenario are those focused on personal comfort and pleasure. But it is perhaps not altogether obvious what would be comforting and pleasant under doomsday conditions.

The upshot is that many types of projects and activities would no longer seem worth pursuing, or as worth pursuing, if we were confronted with the doomsday scenario. Now it is noteworthy that the attractions of these same projects and activities are not similarly undercut by the mere prospect of our own deaths. People cheerfully engage in cancer research and similar activities despite their recognition that the primary payoff of these activities is not likely to be achieved before their own deaths. Yet, if my argument is correct, their motivation to engage in these same activities would be weakened or even completely undermined by the prospect that, in consequence of the earth's destruction, there would be no payoff *after* their deaths. In other words, there are many projects and activities whose importance to us is not diminished by the prospect of our own deaths but would be diminished by the prospect that everyone else will soon die. So if by the afterlife we mean the continuation of human life on earth after our own deaths, then it seems difficult to avoid the conclusion that, in some significant respects, the existence of the afterlife matters more to us than our own continued existence. It matters more to us because it is a condition of other things mattering to us. Without confidence in the existence of the afterlife, many of the things in our own lives that now matter to us would cease to do so or would come to matter less.

Of course, there are many things that are causally necessary in order for our pursuits to matter to us now. Without the presence of oxygen in the atmosphere, for example, nothing would matter to us now because we would not be alive. Similarly, we can imagine that some mineral deficiency in our diet might cause us to lose confidence in the value of our pursuits. Yet we would not conclude that the mineral matters more to us than our own future existence because it is a condition of other things mattering to us now. But the point about our confidence in the afterlife is not merely that it is a causal condition of other things mattering to us now. The continuation of life on earth, unlike the mineral, is something that also matters to us in its own right. And unlike a mineral deficiency, the imminent disappearance of human life on earth would strike us as a *reason* why other things no longer mattered as much. Our belief that humanity was about to disappear would not just be a cause of their ceasing to matter to us.

It is easy to underestimate the significance of this point, at least insofar as it concerns goal-oriented projects like trying to find a cure for cancer. It may seem that, although it is true that such projects would become less important to people who were faced with the doomsday scenario, that is simply because it is pointless or irrational to pursue goals that are known to be unachievable. The goal of reducing the suffering and death caused by cancer would be unachievable under doomsday conditions, so engaging in cancer research would be instrumentally irrational under those conditions. This mundane point about instrumental rationality is all that is needed to explain why people would no longer regard such projects as worth pursuing in the doomsday scenario. But this misconstrues the significance of the example. Granted, it is not surprising that people should lose interest in a goal-oriented project once it is known that the goal of the project is unachievable. What may be surprising, however, is the fact that people are often happy to pursue goals that they do not expect to be achieved until after their own deaths. What the doomsday scenario highlights, in other words, is the extent to which we regard projects as worth undertaking even when the successful completion of those projects is not expected to take place during our own lifetimes. What is significant about the example is what it reveals, not about the familiar role of instrumental rationality in our practical deliberations, but rather about our willingness to harness the resources of instrumental rationality to pursue goals whose achievement will occur only after we are gone.

4.

As I have said, I have so far been concentrating on our general reactions to the doomsday scenario and the general attitudes toward the afterlife that they reveal. However, I want now to consider our more specific reactions to one feature of that scenario, namely, that it involves the sudden, simultaneous deaths of everyone that we love or care about. Since the strength of these reactions can blind us to other aspects of our response to the doomsday scenario, I have so far set them aside in the hope of identifying some of our more general attitudes toward the afterlife. But now I want to return to these more specific reactions, and to see what they add to the general picture that has so far emerged. The salient feature of the doomsday scenario, for these purposes, is that everyone we love who is alive thirty days after our own death will then suddenly be killed. What do our powerful reactions to this prospect tell us about ourselves?

Some elements of our reaction seem obvious and straightforward. We don't want the people we love to die prematurely, whether we are alive to witness their deaths or not. We care deeply about them and their well-being, and not merely about the effects on us of setbacks to their well-being. This is just an example of the non-experiential dimension of our values and concerns. So the knowledge that all the people we love who are still alive thirty days after our own deaths will then die suddenly and more or less prematurely is horrible. That much is clear. Still, I think that there is more to our reaction than this. One way to approach the issue is to ask why it matters to us that at least some people we care about should live on after we die. I take it that most people do regard it as a bad thing if everyone they love or care about dies before they do. Few of us hope to outlive all of our friends and loved ones. Why should this be?

There are, I think, a number of answers to this question and, once again, some of them seem straightforward. The considerations about prematurity just mentioned play a large role, though our preference to predecease at least some of the people we care about may persist even if both we and they are old enough that none of our deaths would qualify as significantly premature. A different kind of consideration is that, if we predecease our loved ones, then we will be spared the pain and grief that we would experience if they died first. Similarly, we will be spared the feelings of loneliness and emptiness and loss to which we may be subject after they are gone. Much better for us if we die first, and they are the ones who have to experience all the unpleasantness. Much as we love them, it seems, we would rather that they suffered in these ways than that we did.

Relatedly, there may be something like a principle of loss minimization at work here. It's bad enough that we will lose our own lives, but there's nothing we can do about that. Given the inevitability of that one final loss, it's better for us that we not experience, in addition, the separate losses of each of the people we care about. It's better if the pain of our separation from them is simply "folded into" the one great calamity of our own deaths. This is essentially a matter of the efficient organization of personal disaster.

But I think that there is something else going on as well. If, at the time of our deaths, there are people alive whom we love or about whom we care deeply, and with whom we have valuable personal relationships, then one effect of our deaths will be to disrupt those relationships. Odd as it may sound, I think that there is something that strikes us as desirable or at any rate comforting about having one's death involve this kind of relational disruption. It is not that the disruptions per se are desirable or comforting, but rather that the prospect of having one's death involve such disruptions affects one's perceived relation to the future. If at the time of one's death one will be a participant in a larger or smaller network of valuable personal relationships, and if the effect of one's death will be to wrench one out of that network, then this can affect one's premortem understanding of the afterlife: the future that will unfold after one is gone. In a certain sense, it personalizes one's relation to that future. Rather than looming simply as a blank eternity of nonexistence, the future can be conceptualized with reference to an ongoing social world in which one retains a social identity. One can imagine oneself into that world simply by imagining the resumption of one's premortem relationships with people who will themselves continue to exist and to remember and care for one. One needn't fear, as many people apparently do, that one will simply be forgotten as soon as one is gone. In fact, to a surprising extent, many people seem to feel that not being remembered is what being "gone" really consists in and, correspondingly, those who are bereaved often feel a powerful imperative not to forget the people they have lost. Faced with the fear of being forgotten, the fact that there are other people who value their relations with you and who will continue to live after you have died makes it possible to feel that you have a place in the social world of the future even if, due to the inconvenient fact of your death, you will not actually be able to take advantage of it. The world of the future becomes, as it were, more like a party one had to leave early and less like a gathering of strangers.

There may be a temptation to protest that the attitudes I have just described are silly or irrational. Death is in fact final, and its finality is not increased if one is forgotten or diminished if one is remembered. Dying, not being forgotten, is what being "gone" consists in. In any case, even if one is remembered for a while, the memories will fade and the people who remember will themselves die soon enough, so it's only a matter of time before nobody who remembers any of us personally will survive. But these protests are beside the point. On the one hand, my aim has not been to show that our attitudes are rational, but, on the other hand, the claim that they are irrational appears to depend on just the kind of experientialism that I have tried to discredit. The fact is that it does matter to us to have other people we care about live on after we die, and it also matters to us to be remembered, at least for a while. These things matter to us, I have argued, partly because they help to personalize our relation to the future. One reason why we react so strongly to the doomsday scenario is that it seems to render our own relation to the future incurably bleak. We are used to the idea that we ourselves will not be a part of the future after our deaths. In the doomsday scenario, we must reconcile ourselves to the fact that nobody we care about will be a part of the future either, and that fact, I have suggested, makes the future itself seem more alien, forbidding, empty. It is idle to protest that, if we were rational, it would seem just as empty to us even if the doomsday scenario were suspended and we could be assured that the people we care about would live normal life spans. Why, the protester asks, should we take comfort in their survival given that they too will die soon enough? But the vantage point from which these attitudes are judged irrational enjoys no special privilege or authority. If the idea that some of the people we care about will live on is one of the things that enables us to make our peace with the future, and if, in reacting that way, we make no error of reasoning and rely on no false belief, then the basis for criticism is obscure.

I should say something at this point about children. I have been arguing that our participation in valued relationships with people we hope will outlive us transforms our attitudes toward the future after we are gone. It is obvious that, for people who have children, their relationships with their children have a special role to play here. The desire for a personalized relation to the future is one of the many reasons why people attach such importance to those relationships, and why the loss of a child is one of the most devastating things that can happen to a person. But I have deliberately avoided making children central to the argument, because I do not think that the desire for a personalized relation to the future is limited to people with children, nor do I think that relationships with children are the only kinds of personal relationships that can help to satisfy that desire. Those who tend to think about things in the terms of evolutionary biology will point out that it is all too easy to explain in those terms why people should be motivated to have biological descendants who will survive them. For the purposes of my argument, however, these explanations are doubly irrelevant. They are irrelevant, first, because the relationships that can help to satisfy the desire for a personalized relation to the future are not limited to relationships with one's biological descendants. And they are irrelevant, second, because I am interested simply in the fact that we have that desire and in its relations to others of our attitudes. An evolutionary explanation of the desire would not show that we do not have it, or that it is not a genuine desire, any more than an evolutionary explanation of our perceptual abilities would show that we do not really have those abilities or an evolutionary explanation of parental love would show that it is not really love.

At this point, let me pause to summarize the arguments I have presented so far. First, I have argued that our reactions to the doomsday scenario highlight some general features of the phenomenon of human valuing, which I have referred to as its nonexperientialist, nonconsequentialist, and conservative dimensions. We do not care only about our own experiences. We do not care only that the best consequences should come to pass. And we do want the things that we value to be sustained and preserved over time. Second, I have argued that the afterlife matters to us, and in more than one way. What happens after our deaths matters to us in its own right and, in addition, our confidence that there will be an afterlife is a condition of many other things mattering to us here and now. Third, I have argued that the doomsday scenario highlights some of our attitudes toward time, particularly our impulse to personalize our relation to the future.

5.

Let me now try to expand on these provisional conclusions. As I have noted, death poses a problem for our conservatism about value. We want to act in ways that will help preserve and sustain the things that we value, but death marks the end of our ability to do this. As I have also noted, death poses a problem for our relationship with time. We want to personalize our relation to the future, yet for most of the future we will no longer be alive. I have already made some suggestions about how we attempt to deal with these two problems as individuals. In the first case, we take steps while we are alive to ensure that others will act so as to sustain those values after our deaths. In the second case, our participation in valued personal relationships with people whom we hope will outlive us transforms our attitudes toward the future after we are gone.

These responses are important but they have their limits. Many people supplement them by participating in group-based responses as well. One of the most important ways in which people attempt to preserve and sustain their values, for example, is by participating in traditions that themselves support those values. Traditions are, as I have said elsewhere,[5] human practices whose organizing purpose is to preserve what is valued beyond the life span of any single individual or generation. They are collaborative, multigenerational enterprises devised by human beings precisely to satisfy the deep human impulse to preserve what is valued. In subscribing to a tradition that embodies values one embraces, or whose own value one embraces, one seeks to ensure the survival over time of what one values. Although traditions are not themselves guaranteed to survive, a flourishing tradition will typically have far greater resources to devote to the preservation of values, and very different kinds of resources, than any single individual is likely to have. So by participating in traditions that embody the values to which they are committed, individuals can leverage their own personal efforts to ensure the survival of those values. In addition, they can think of themselves as being, along with their fellow traditionalists, the custodians of values that will eventually be transmitted to future generations. In this sense, participation in a tradition is not only an expression of our natural conservatism about values but also a way of achieving a *value-based* relation to those who come after us. We can think of our successors as people who will share our values, and ourselves as having custodial responsibility for the values that will someday be theirs.[6]

5. "The Normativity of Tradition," in *Equality and Tradition*, ch. 11, 287–311.

6. By the same token, of course, participation in a tradition also enables us to feel that we have inherited values handed down to us by others, and in this way

Our efforts to personalize our relations to the future also take group-based forms. In addition to participating in valued personal relations with other specific individuals, at least some of whom we hope will survive us, many people also belong to, and value their membership in, communal or national groups, most of whose members they do not know personally. Often it becomes important to them that these groups should survive after they are gone. Indeed, for some people, the survival of the community or the clan or the people or the nation has an importance that is comparable to—or nearly comparable to—the importance they attach to the survival of their loved ones. Similarly, the prospect that the group will survive after they as individuals are gone serves to personalize their relation to the future in much the same way as does the prospect that their own loved ones will survive. Even if, by contrast to the latter case, the survival of the group does not mean that one will personally be remembered, it nevertheless gives one license to imagine oneself as retaining a social identity in the world of the future. In neither case does this involve the false belief that one will actually survive one's death. It merely allows one to think that if, contrary to fact, one did survive, one would remain socially at home in the world. If I am right, this is a surprisingly powerful and comforting thought for many people. It provides assurance that, socially speaking, at least, the world of the future is not an altogether alien place. Max Weber may have been right to say that we live in a disenchanted world,[7] but I believe that many people who find the lack of enchantment tolerable or even welcome nevertheless remain troubled by, and go to some lengths to preclude, the prospect of a depersonalized world. The group-based strategy for personalizing one's relation to the future offers some clear advantages as compared with reliance solely

makes it possible for us to achieve a value-based relation to those who came before us. For discussion, see "The Normativity of Tradition," 305.

7. See Max Weber, "Science as a Vocation," in David Owen and Tracy Strong eds., *The Vocation Lectures* (Indianapolis, IN: Hackett, 2004), 1–31.

on the survival of particular individuals, since—at the risk of bela-boring the obvious—groups can enjoy much greater longevity than can any single individual.

I have described separately the group-based solutions people use to help solve two different problems posed by death: the problem of preserving our values and the problem of establishing a personalized relation to the future. But, except for heuristic purposes, it is artificial to think of the two types of solution as being mutually independent, for to a very great extent they overlap. The value-sustaining tradi-tions that help to solve the first problem must themselves be sus-tained by communities of people, and the communal or national groups that help to solve the second problem are normally unified by their shared allegiance to a set of values. So in availing oneself of one of these solutions, one is normally availing oneself of the other as well. In relying on a tradition to help preserve our values, we are seeking to create a future whose inhabitants will share with us some of the commitments that matter most to us. To that extent, the con-servative impulse, although it is naturally thought of as embodying an attitude toward the past, is also, perforce, an impulse to create a personalized relation to the future. Conversely, in seeking to ensure the survival of communal or national groups that matter to us, we are seeking to create a future in which the values we have historically shared with other members of the group will continue to endure. To that extent, the impulse to personalize our relation to the future is also, perforce, an impulse to conserve our values, and in that respect it embodies an attitude toward the past. Ultimately, both solutions are part of a unified attempt to defend and extend the coherence and integrity of our selves and our values over time, in the face of the apparently insuperable problems posed by our deaths. Needless to say, these efforts can never be completely successful. Only survival could give us all of what we want, and survival is not an option. So, like the biblical Moses denied access to the Promised Land, we stand gazing through the lens of shared values and history toward a future we will not enter.

6.

Of course, the doomsday scenario thwarts the group-based solutions as decisively as it thwarts their more individualistic counterparts, since the traditions and groups upon which those solutions rely will also be destroyed when the doomsday collision takes place. This raises questions about the motivational sustainability under doomsday conditions of a whole new range of projects, in addition to those surveyed earlier. For example, many people have projects that are defined in relation to a particular tradition. Some of these projects may be meant to enhance or contribute to or enrich or sustain the tradition. Others may simply take up options that the tradition itself makes available, and which make sense only within the framework of the tradition and its practices, history, and self-understanding. Similarly, many people have projects that are defined in relation to a particular community or nation or people. Some of these projects may be meant to contribute to the flourishing of the group or its institutions. Others may be designed to help the group realize certain of its aims and aspirations. Again, still others may simply take up options that the group makes available and which make sense only within the framework of its practices and self-understanding.

Would projects of these kinds retain their motivational appeal under doomsday conditions? In other words, would pursuing such projects continue to seem important to individuals who had previously been committed to them if those individuals knew that the tradition or community that was the focus or the source of their project would be destroyed thirty days after their own death? Or would it then seem to them less important to persevere with their projects? Would they see less reason to do so? The answer, of course, may depend on the nature of the particular project in question. And there might well be some variation from individual to individual. But it seems plausible that many tradition-dependent and group-dependent projects would come to seem less important to people.

This seems especially true of projects whose explicit aim either was or was dependent on the long-term survival and flourishing of a particular tradition or group, for those projects would now be known in advance to be doomed to failure. And so we have here another important range of examples of the phenomenon noted earlier, in which our confidence in the existence of an afterlife is a condition of our projects continuing to matter to us while we are alive.

7.

However, these examples may create or reinforce the impression that, to the extent that our confidence in the existence of an afterlife has this kind of importance for us, it is really the postmortem survival of specific individuals or groups that we care about. I have already noted that one effect of the doomsday scenario is to highlight the importance we attach to the survival of the particular people who matter to us, and we have now seen that the survival of particular groups and traditions may be of comparable importance, at least for some people. In general, the desire to personalize our relation to the future, which is one of the desires whose tacit power is revealed by the doomsday scenario, is a desire that seems to require *particularistic* satisfaction. What enables us to establish a personalized relation to the future, it seems, is our confidence in the survival after our deaths of some particular people we love or particular groups or traditions to which we are committed. And this may tempt us to conclude that the afterlife that matters to us is the afterlife of those people alone.

Yet this conclusion is too hasty. Recall that, when first discussing the doomsday scenario, I deliberately concentrated on our more general reactions to the scenario, and provisionally set aside our more specific responses to the prospect that our own loved ones would die. The aim was to prevent the power of those more particularistic responses from obscuring other, less conspicuous elements of our reaction. So in discussing various projects that might come to matter less to us, I deliberately focused on projects, such as the project of engaging in cancer research, that lacked any obvious dependence on particularistic loyalties or affections. To the extent that pursuing that project would come to seem less important to a researcher confronting the doomsday scenario, it is not because the scenario involves the imminent death of particular people she loves or the destruction of particular groups to which she belongs and is committed. If that is correct, then our concern for the existence of an afterlife is not solely a concern for the survival of particular people or groups.

This conclusion can be strengthened. It is clear that the prospective destruction of the particular people we care about would be sufficient for us to react with horror to an impending global disaster, and that the elimination of human life as a whole would not be necessary. But, surprisingly perhaps, it seems that the reverse is also true. The imminent disappearance of human life would be sufficient for us to react with horror even if it would not involve the premature death of any of our loved ones. This, it seems to me, is one lesson of P. D. James's novel *The Children of Men*,[8] which was published in 1992, and a considerably altered version of which was made into a film in 2006 by the Mexican filmmaker Alfonso Cuarón. The premise of James's novel, which is set in 2021, is that human beings have become infertile, with no recorded birth having occurred in more than twenty-five years. The human race thus faces the prospect of imminent extinction as the last generation born gradually dies out.[9] The plot of the book revolves around the

8. James's novel was first published by Faber and Faber (London, 1992). Page references, which will be given parenthetically in the text, are to the Vintage Books edition published by Random House in 2006.

9. On July 28, 2009, *New York Times* columnist David Brooks, citing a brief item posted by Tyler Cowen a few days earlier on the *Marginal Revolution* blog, http://www.marginalrevolution.com/marginalrevolution/2009/07/mass-

unexpected pregnancy of an English woman and the ensuing attempts of a small group of people to ensure the safety and freedom of the woman and her baby. For our purposes, however, what is relevant is not this central plot line, with its overtones of Christian allegory, but rather James's imaginative dystopian portrayal of life on earth prior to the discovery of the redemptive pregnancy. And what is notable is that her asteroid-free variant of the doomsday scenario does not require anyone to die prematurely. It is entirely compatible with every living person having a normal life span. So if we imagine ourselves inhabiting James's infertile world and we try to predict what our reactions would be to the imminent disappearance of human life on earth, it is clear that those reactions would not include any feelings about the premature deaths of our loved ones, for no such deaths would occur (or at any rate, none would occur as an essential feature of James's scenario itself). To the extent that we would nevertheless find the prospect of human extinction disturbing or worse, our imagined reaction lacks the particularistic character of a concern for the survival of our loved ones. Indeed, there would be no identifiable people at all who could serve as the focus of our concern, except, of course, insofar as the elimination of a human afterlife gave us reason to feel concern for ourselves and for others now alive, despite its having no implications whatsoever about our own mortality or theirs.

sterilization.html#comments, wrote an article titled "The Power of Posterity," in which he considered what would happen if *half* the world's population were sterilized as a result of a "freak solar event," http://www.nytimes.com/2009/07/28/opinion/28brooks.html?scp=1&sq=power%20of%20posterity&st=cse. Although some of Brooks's speculations evoke, albeit rather stridently, some of the themes of James's novel (and of these lectures), the proviso that only half the world's population becomes infertile leads him ultimately in a different direction. Neither Cowen nor Brooks cites *The Children of Men*, although online reader comments responding to Cowen's blog post and to Brooks's column both note the connection.

Of course, the infertility scenario would mean that many groups and traditions would die out sooner than they otherwise would have done, and this would presumably be a source of particularistic distress for those with group-based or traditional allegiances. Still, because the infertility scenario suppresses the influence of any particularistic concern for individuals, it is more effective than the original doomsday scenario in highlighting something that I think is evident despite the persistence of group-based particularistic responses. What is evident is that, for all the power of the particularistic elements in our reactions to the catastrophe scenarios we have been discussing, there is also another powerful element that is at work, namely, the impact that the imminent end of humanity as such would have on us.

8.

What exactly that impact would be is, of course, a matter of speculation, as indeed are all the other hypothetical reactions to imagined disasters that we have been discussing. The speculations of P. D. James and Alfonso Cuarón have no special authority, apart from the authority that comes from having reflected seriously about the topic and from wanting to create fictional portrayals that audiences would find plausible enough to compel their interest and attention. Their speculations differ from each other in certain respects, just as my speculations may differ from theirs, and yours may differ from mine. Having said that, however, I hope it will not strike you as outlandish when I add that, like them, I find it plausible to suppose that such a world would be a world characterized by widespread apathy, anomie, and despair; by the erosion of social institutions and social solidarity; by the deterioration of the physical environment; and by a pervasive loss of conviction about the value or point of many activities.

In James's version of the story, an authoritarian government in Britain has largely avoided the savage anarchy that prevails in other parts of the world, and it has achieved a measure of popular support by promising people "freedom from fear, freedom from want, freedom from boredom" (97), though the last of these promises proves difficult to keep in the face of mounting indifference toward most previously attractive activities. This indifference extends not only to those activities with an obvious orientation toward the future but also to those, like sex, that offer immediate gratification and might therefore have seemed likely to retain their popularity in an infertile world, but which turn out not to be exempt from the growing apathy. The government, hoping that the infertility may yet prove temporary, has to encourage continued interest in sex through the establishment of "national porn shops" (7). Theo Faron, the Oxford don who serves as James's protagonist and sometimes narrator says, describing people's reactions once they became convinced that the infertility was irreversible, that suicide increased and that "those who lived gave way to the almost universal negativism, what the French named *ennui universel*. It came upon us like an insidious disease; indeed, it was a disease, with its soon-familiar symptoms of lassitude, depression, ill-defined malaise, a readiness to give way to minor infections, a perpetual disabling headache" (9). The exceptions to this syndrome are those who are protected "by a lack of imagination" or by an "egotism so powerful that no external catastrophe can prevail against it" (9). And although Theo himself continues to fight against the ennui by trying to take pleasure in books, music, food, wine, and nature, he finds that pleasure "now comes so rarely and, when it does, is...indistinguishable from pain" (9). "Without the hope of posterity," he says, "for our race if not for ourselves, without the assurance that we being dead yet live, all pleasures of the mind and senses sometimes seem to me no more than pathetic and crumbling defences shored up against our ruins" (9).

To the extent that all this is persuasive, it suggests a significant increase in the range of activities whose perceived value might be threatened by the recognition that life on earth was about to come to an end. I have already noted several different types of activities that would be threatened by that prospect. First, there are some projects, such as cancer research or the development of new seismic safety techniques, which would be threatened because they have a goal-oriented character, and the goals they seek to achieve would straightforwardly be thwarted if the human race were imminently to disappear. Second, there are some projects, including creative projects of various kinds, which would be threatened because they tacitly depend for their perceived success on their reception by an imagined future audience, and the end of human life would mean the disappearance of audiences. Third, there are a large number of activities, including but not limited to those associated with participation in a tradition, which would be threatened because their point is in part to sustain certain values and practices over time, and the end of human life would mark the defeat of all such efforts. Fourth, and relatedly, there are activities that would be threatened because they are aimed at promoting the survival and flourishing of particular national or communal groups, and those aims too would be doomed to frustration if human life were about to come to an end.

In addition, however, James's narrative encourages us to think that there are other, less obvious sorts of activities whose perceived value might also be threatened in an infertile world. It suggests, more specifically, that many activities whose rewards seem independent of those activities' contribution to any longer term process or undertaking might nevertheless be vulnerable in this way. Even such things as the enjoyment of nature; the appreciation of literature, music, and the visual arts; the achievement of knowledge and understanding; and the appetitive pleasures of food, drink, and sex might be affected. This suggestion is likely to strike some people as implausible, and it may well be that individuals' attitudes toward these activities, if they were actually confronted with the infertility scenario, would be more variable and idiosyncratic than their attitudes toward activities in the other categories I have mentioned.

Still, I believe that James's speculations about the effects of the infertility scenario on people's attitudes toward these dimensions of human experience are suggestive. They give imaginative expression to the not implausible idea that the imminent disappearance of human life would exert a generally depressive effect on people's motivations and on their confidence in the value of their activities—that it would reduce their capacity for enthusiasm and for wholehearted and joyful activity across a very wide front. The same speculations also invite us to consider a slightly more specific possibility. We normally understand such things as the appreciation of literature and the arts, the acquisition of knowledge and understanding of the world around us, and the enjoyment of the appetitive pleasures to be constituents of the good life. This means that we take a certain view about the place of these goods in a human life as a whole. But James's speculations invite us to consider the possibility that our conception of "a human life as a whole" relies on an implicit understanding of such a life as itself occupying a place in an ongoing human history, in a temporally extended chain of lives and generations. If this is so, then, perhaps, we cannot simply take it for granted that the activity of, say, reading *The Catcher in the Rye*, or trying to understand quantum mechanics, or even eating an excellent meal would have the same significance for people, or offer them the same rewards, in a world that was known to be deprived of a human future. We cannot assume that we know what the constituents of a good life would be in such a world, nor can we even be confident that there is something that we would be prepared to count as a good life.

9.

For my purposes, however, it is not necessary that all the details of James's version of the story should be found convincing, nor is it necessary to arrive at a settled conclusion about the exact range of activities whose perceived value would be eroded in an infertile world. All that is necessary is to suppose that, in such a world, people would lose confidence in the value of many sorts of activities, would cease to see reason to engage in many familiar sorts of pursuits, and would become emotionally detached from many of those activities and pursuits. As I have said, this seems plausible to me, and I hope that it will seem plausible to you too. So let me just stipulate that this assumption—which I will call "the afterlife conjecture"—is true. I take the afterlife conjecture to have implications of a number of different kinds. Perhaps the most striking of these has to do with the nature and limits of our egoism. We are all rightly impressed by the power and extent of our self-concern, and even the most ardent defenders of morality feel the need to argue for what Thomas Nagel called "the possibility of altruism" in the face of the more or less universal assumption that our default motivations are powerfully self-interested.[10] But consider this. Every single person now alive will be dead in the not-too-distant future. This fact is universally accepted and is not seen as remarkable, still less as an impending catastrophe. There are no crisis meetings of world leaders to consider what to do about it, no outbreaks of mass hysteria, no outpourings of grief, no demands for action. This does not mean that individuals do not fear their own deaths. To the contrary, many people are terrified of death and wish desperately to survive for as long as possible. Despite this, neither the recognition of their own mortality nor the prospect that everyone now alive will soon die leads most people to conclude that few of their worldly activities are important or worth pursuing. Of course, many people do find themselves, through bad luck or lack of opportunity, engaged in activities that do not seem to them worthwhile. Similarly, many individuals do at some point in their lives experience episodes of depression or despair, and the tragedy of suicide remains an all too common occurrence. But relatively little of this, I venture to say, is explained by reference to the impact on people of the recognition

10. Thomas Nagel, *The Possibility of Altruism* (Oxford: Clarendon Press, 1970).

that all the earth's current inhabitants will someday die. Not only is that fact not regarded as a catastrophe, it is not even on anybody's list of the major problems facing the world.

You may be tempted to say that it is not seen as a major problem because it is known to be inevitable. People have accepted the fact that everyone now alive will die and that nothing can be done about it. Yet in the infertile world, the disappearance of the human race is also widely understood to be inevitable, but it *is* regarded as a catastrophe. In James's vivid depiction, it is regarded as a catastrophe whose prospect precipitates an unprecedented global crisis and exerts a profoundly depressive effect on many familiar human motivations. And if, as the afterlife conjecture supposes, at least the core of this depiction is accurate, the implication seems clear. In certain concrete functional and motivational respects, the fact that we and everyone we love will cease to exist matters less to us than would the nonexistence of future people whom we do not know and who, indeed, have no determinate identities. Or to put it more positively, the coming into existence of people we do not know and love matters more to us than our own survival and the survival of the people we do know and love. Even allowing for the likelihood that some portion of our concern for these future people is a concern for the survival of particular groups with which we specially identify, this is a remarkable fact which should get more attention than it does in thinking about the nature and limits of our personal egoism.[11]

---

11. Here it seems worth mentioning Dan Moller's interesting argument to the effect that the participants in loving relationships have much less importance for one another than we normally suppose. Moller bases his argument on empirical findings which suggest that the participants in such relationships are surprisingly resilient in the face of the loss of a partner or spouse. There is a superficial similarity between Moller's claim about the relative unimportance that spouses and partners have for one another and my claim that, in some respects, our own survival and the survival of the people we love matters less to us than does the existence of future people. Yet the two claims are in fact quite

It may seem that this is too hasty a conclusion to draw. Although people in the infertility scenario do come to view the disappearance of the human race as inevitable, this involves a change in their expectations. As I have described the scenario, most of these people begin life thinking that humanity will endure and learn only later that it will not. So the infertility scenario involves a drastic change of expectations for them. By contrast, we all grow up understanding that we will someday die, and we have formed our expectations accordingly. Perhaps the differing responses to which I have called attention are evidence not of the limits of our egoism but merely of the power of disappointed expectations. If people had grown up knowing that they were the last generation of humans, perhaps this would have no greater impact on them than the prospect of our own deaths has on us. But I find this difficult to believe. I agree, of course, that the change in expectations might itself have a dramatic effect on people's attitudes. It would surely have a dramatic effect on our attitudes if we grew up thinking that we were immortal and discovered our own mortality only in middle age. But I do not think that those who grew up knowing that they were the last generation of human beings would be exempt from the phenomena that I have described. To me it seems implausible that the effect of this grim piece of knowledge would be to support their confidence in the value of their activities. It seems at least as plausible that, in contrast to those who discovered only later in life that they were the

different. Moller's concern is with our reactions to actual losses while mine is with our reactions to prospective losses. Since we can have no reactions at all to our own actual deaths, Moller focuses exclusively on our reactions to the deaths of other people one loves, whereas I am concerned with the prospective loss not only of one's loved ones but also of one's own life. And whereas my point is that the relevant prospective reactions reveal some limits of our egoism, he takes our reactions to actual losses as evidencing a kind of emotional shallowness—a failure to register the true value of our loved ones and our relationships with them—which we have reason to regret. See Dan Moller, "Love and Death," *Journal of Philosophy* 104 (2007): 301–16.

last generation, those who grew up with this understanding would simply lack such confidence from the outset.

It may be objected that there is another, simpler explanation for the differing responses to which I have called attention, and this explanation also does not support any conclusions about the limits of our egoism. The fact that everyone now alive will soon die is not regarded as a catastrophe, and does not precipitate a global crisis, because it poses no threat to society itself. By contrast, the infertility scenario would mean the end of society, and so of course it would be viewed as catastrophic. This fact is unremarkable and shows nothing one way or another about the extent of our egoism. But this objection misses the point. It is true that the infertility scenario would mean the end of society, and it is not wrong to say that that is why it would be regarded as a catastrophe. However, under the terms of that scenario, "the end of society" would neither cause nor result from any change in the mortality or longevity of anyone now alive. From the perspective of those now living, the only difference between the infertility scenario and the mundane circumstance that everyone now living will soon die is that, in the infertility scenario, it is also true that no as yet unborn people will come into existence. So in finding that scenario but not the mundane prospect of universal death catastrophic, one is evincing a level of concern about the nonexistence of future people that exceeds one's concern about the mortality of existing people. Characterizing this heightened level of concern as a concern about "the end of society" doesn't change this fact. It merely redescribes it. And however one describes it, it continues to suggest some striking limits to our personal egoism.

A different kind of objection would be to concede that our reaction to the infertility scenario evinces concern about the nonexistence of future people, but to argue that this concern can itself be explained as a manifestation of, rather than a departure from, our egoism. For the youngest among us, it may be said, the infertility scenario implies that there would be nobody alive to support or care for them when they became old. In the final years of their lives, there would effectively be no economy; no goods would be produced or services provided. As the last generation of humans on earth, they would have no successors to provide the emotional, material, or medical support that they would require. So the infertility scenario would be, from a purely self-interested point of view, a disaster for them, and it would also alter for the worse their relations with other living generations. It might, for example, make them less willing to provide support for their own elders, and those elders might in turn be less willing to provide support for *their* elders, and so on. The result would be a ripple effect in which the disastrous implications for the youngest people would be passed up the generational ladder and would ultimately include everyone in society. In consequence, the infertility scenario might well be viewed as catastrophic by all of those now living, but only for instrumental, self-interested reasons.

This objection clearly has some merit, but I do not believe that it is the whole story. If it were, it would imply that, provided that the comfort of the youngest generation in their final years could be assured (perhaps by providing with them with thoughtfully preprogrammed caregiver robots[12]), then they, and by implication the rest of the living, could contemplate the imminent end of human life on earth with equanimity, or at least with no less equanimity than that with which people now contemplate their own deaths. But this strikes me as incredible. To me it seems clear, as I hope it will to you, that the infertility scenario would be viewed as catastrophic even if it were known in advance that it would not have any negative

12. When I first wrote this, I thought that I was describing something purely in the realm of science fiction, but that turns out not to be true. See, for example, Daniel Bartz, "Toyota Sees Robotic Nurses in Your Lonely Final Years," *Wired*, Jan. 19, 2010, http://www.wired.com/gadgetlab/2010/01/toyota-sees-robotic-nurses-in-your-lonely-final-years/, and, in the same vein, Calum MacLeod, "A Glimpse of the Future: Robots Aid Japan's Elderly Residents," *USA Today*, Nov. 5, 2009, http://www.usatoday.com/tech/news/robotics/2009-11-04-japan-robots_N.htm.

effect on either the physical comfort or the longevity of any living person.[13] That, at any rate, is what the afterlife conjecture supposes. In the second lecture, I will explore some of the additional implications of this conjecture, which seem to me far-reaching.

13. Is it the survival of human beings that matters to us or the survival of people (persons)? In the text I treat the two ideas as equivalent, but many philosophers suppose that, in principle, there might be members of nonhuman species who qualified as persons. Suppose we knew that the disappearance of human beings was imminent but that it would be accompanied by the sudden emergence on earth of a new species of nonhuman persons. Would that be sufficient to restore our confidence in the value of our activities? If so, then perhaps it is the existence of people rather than the existence of human beings that matters to us. If not, then perhaps it is the survival of human beings in particular that we care about. But perhaps it is neither of these things. Perhaps what matters is the survival of people who share our values and seek to perpetuate our traditions and ways of life. If so, then the survival of human beings is neither necessary nor sufficient. Nonhuman persons with our values might do just as well. And human beings without our values would not help.

To the extent that these are questions about how we would react in various highly counterfactual circumstances, they are empirical questions that are extremely difficult to answer. My own view, as should be clear from the text, is that most of us do hope that future generations will share our most important values, but that the survival of humanity also matters to us in a way that is not exhausted by this concern. It is important to us that human beings should survive even though we know that their values and cultures will change in ways that we cannot anticipate and some of which we would not welcome. The future existence of nonhuman persons might provide some consolation if human beings did not survive, though a lot would depend on what exactly this new species was like and how its history was related to ours. In any case, though, I doubt whether the emergence of the new species would seem to us just as good as the survival of our own. That is in part because, despite what the terminology might suggest, I doubt whether we would view the existence of these nonhuman persons as providing us with the basis for what I have called "a personalized relation to the future." In short, what I take the arguments of these lectures to show is that the survival of human persons matters greatly to us, although it is not the only thing that matters to us, and although there are other imaginable things that might provide some consolation if we knew that human persons were about to disappear.

Lecture 2: The Afterlife (Part II)

1.

The first topic I want to address in this lecture concerns the precise way in which what matters depends on what I have been calling the "afterlife." We have seen that without confidence that there will be such an afterlife—without confidence that others will live on after we ourselves have died—many of the things that now matter to us would cease to do so or would come to matter to us less. This was evident from the original doomsday scenario, and the infertility scenario made it clear that the importance to us of the afterlife does not derive solely from a concern for the survival of our loved ones. But we can distinguish among three different theses about the way in which what matters depends on the afterlife. The first thesis, which is the one I have been defending, holds that what matters *to us* implicitly depends on *our confidence* in the existence of the afterlife. We may refer to this as the *attitudinal* dependency thesis, because it asserts the dependence of some of our attitudes on others of our attitudes. It asserts that if we lost confidence in the existence of the afterlife, then many of the things that now matter to us would come to matter to us less, in the sense that we would see less reason to engage with them, would become less emotionally invested in them, and would be less convinced of their value or worth.

However, this attitudinal dependence itself implies that these things would become less important *to us* partly because, without confidence in the afterlife, we would see them as less important or valuable *simpliciter*. And this suggests that we accept a second dependency thesis, namely, that their mattering *simpliciter* depends on the actual existence of the afterlife, and not merely on our confidence in it. If we ceased to see our activities as valuable because we became convinced that there would be no afterlife, then the prospect of taking a drug that would induce a false belief in the existence of the afterlife would not, prospectively, convince us that the activities were about to become valuable again. For what we would believe, prior to taking the drug, was that those activities being valuable depends not on our belief in the afterlife, but on the actual existence of the afterlife. To the extent that we would have these reactions, this confirms that we accept an *evaluative* dependency thesis, which asserts that things matter or are valuable *simpliciter* only if there is in fact an afterlife.

Moreover, if our valuing something consists partly in our belief that it is valuable *simpliciter*, and if we tacitly accept that something's being valuable *simpliciter* depends on the actual existence of the afterlife, then it seems to follow that we accept still another dependency thesis, according to which our valuing something, or its mattering *to us*, also depends in an important respect on the actual existence of the afterlife and not merely on our confidence in it. Suppose that our activities ceased to matter to us because we believed that there would be no afterlife. Suppose now that an all-powerful being offered to make things matter to us again in either of two ways. Either the being could restore both the existence of the afterlife and our fully justified belief in it, or it could simply give us a drug that would induce in us a false belief in the afterlife. I take it that we would not regard these as equally good ways of making things matter to us. We might feel that if we took the drug, then, although our activities would in fact come to matter to us, we would be mistaken in valuing or attaching importance to them. There would not be good reasons for them to matter to us, and there would be good reasons for them not to. Perhaps we might even express the point by saying that, if we took the drug, then our activities would *seem* to matter to us but they wouldn't *really* matter to us. To the extent that we would have these reactions, we appear to accept a *justificatory* dependency thesis, which holds that we are justified in attaching importance to things, or that there is good reason for them to matter to us, only if there is an afterlife.

So we can distinguish among three different dependency theses: attitudinal, evaluative, and justificatory. The afterlife conjecture, which asserts that people faced with the infertility scenario would lose confidence in the value of many of their activities, provides direct support for the truth of the attitudinal dependency thesis but not for the evaluative or justificatory theses. Instead, by providing direct support for the truth of the attitudinal dependency thesis, it provides indirect support for the *ascription to us* of the evaluative and justificatory dependency theses. It suggests that we tacitly take things to matter, and take ourselves to be justified in attaching importance to things, only insofar as there is in fact an afterlife, and not merely insofar as we believe that there is.

This leaves open the possibility that the evaluative and justificatory theses are nevertheless false. It is possible that, although we would lose confidence in the value of our activities if we were confronted with the infertility scenario, we would be making a mistake in so doing. Our valuable activities would remain just as valuable even if the disappearance of humanity were imminent. To the extent that we thought otherwise when confronted with the scenario, we would be wrong. In fact, this doesn't seem to me like a very plausible thing to say with regard to goal-oriented projects like finding a cure for cancer or developing new techniques for improving seismic safety. It seems equally implausible as applied to projects aimed at ensuring the survival and flourishing of a particular community or tradition. With respect to other activities, I am less certain. I can see some appeal in the suggestion that, for example, intellectual activities would continue to be just as valuable even if humanity's disappearance were imminent and even if, in such circumstances, many of us would lose confidence in the value of those activities. But I can also see some appeal in the contrary suggestion. Suppose that when confronted with the infertility scenario, a historian were to lose confidence in the value of conducting his planned research on Bulgarian military history. Or suppose that a political philosopher were to lose confidence in the value of writing additional articles about the relation between liberty and equality or about the correct interpretation of John Rawls's difference principle. Rather than assuming that the historian and the philosopher would be making a mistake, we might instead conclude that their reactions teach us something unexpected about the importance of our activities. In reflecting on their anticipated loss of confidence, in other words, it is tempting to say that we *discover* something, namely, that, to a greater extent than we may have realized, the actual value of our activities depends on their place in an ongoing human history.

There are, however, exceptions to the patterns of dependency I have been describing. Not all the things that matter to us are dependent on our confidence in the existence of the afterlife. Obvious exceptions might include such things as relief from extreme pain. Even in an infertile world, it seems plausible to suppose that it would be important to people to be free from severe pain and, if they were experiencing such pain, it would be important to them to have it end. It does not seem likely that the disappearance of the afterlife would make this matter less to them. Nor, similarly, does it seem likely that friendship and other close personal relations would cease to matter to people. Indeed, it may seem that they would come to matter even more, although the issue is complicated. On the one hand, we would expect that personal relationships would provide a sense of solidarity in the face of the looming catastrophe and, for that reason, that they would be an especially important source of comfort and solace. On the other hand, friendships are normally nourished by the engagement of each of the participants with valued activities, interests, and pursuits outside of the friendship itself. The effects on any given friendship of a mutual loss of confidence in the value of many of the participants' other activities are difficult to predict. Moreover, friendship, like the other goods discussed earlier, is something that we normally think of as having a certain place in a human life as a whole. So if, as I have speculated, one effect of the infertility scenario would be to undermine our ideas about the shape and even the possibility of a good human life, then this might affect people's attitudes toward their friendships and their friends in ways that are also difficult to predict. Still, it seems plausible to suppose that friendships and other personal relationships would retain considerable importance for people in an infertile world.

A different kind of example has to do with the existence of the afterlife itself. It is an implication of the argument I have been developing that the afterlife would itself continue to matter to people in an infertile world. And the fact that there was to be no afterlife would matter greatly to them. After all, the whole premise of the infertility scenario is that the elimination of the afterlife would have profound effects on people's emotions, motivations, and understanding of their reasons, and this implies that the afterlife (and its elimination) would continue to matter very much to them. But if this is right, it constitutes an important exception to the idea that what matters to us or seems important to us depends on our confidence in the existence of the afterlife. It shows that the importance to us of the afterlife does not itself depend on our confidence in the existence of the afterlife. Nor, it seems, does it depend on the actual existence of the afterlife. If we contemplate the prospect that there will be no afterlife, this will not lead us to conclude that the existence of the afterlife either does not or should not matter to us. In short, the afterlife matters to us whether there will be an afterlife or not.

Finally, let me mention an example of an altogether different kind. Consider the question of why, in ordinary circumstances, people play games. I have in mind games played by amateurs, for recreational purposes, with no prospect of monetary reward. And for simplicity let us focus on games that require relatively little in the way of special talents or skills. Part of the answer, it seems to me, is that games create what might be thought of as self-contained bubbles of significance. The rules of a game determine what matters or is important to the players within the context of the game. The players understand that the things that matter to them in the context of the game are of no importance to them outside that context. If I am playing Monopoly, then my ability to use some of my play money to put a little "hotel" on a square of the board that I am said to "own" may matter a lot to me, even though I know perfectly well that it has no context-independent significance for me at all. And things that are of great importance to me outside the context of the game are irrelevant within it. My attempts to buy an actual house in which to live may matter greatly to me, but they don't even register as relevant in the Monopoly world. In that sense, games establish artificial contexts in which things that otherwise lack importance to the participants are taken by them to matter greatly. To play the game is to inhabit this artificial context for a period of time, and to accept and internalize, at least temporarily, its conception of what is important and what matters.

It is an interesting question why people find it appealing to do this. Given that there are things that really matter to us, why do we find it enjoyable to enter an artificial context in which things that do not otherwise matter to us are treated as if they did? Of course, not everyone finds it enjoyable to play games. Some people actually have an aversion to doing so, and for some of those people the aversion may derive precisely from the fact that the contexts of value or importance established by games are artificial. In other words, it may derive from the fact that the participants are expected to act as if things that don't really matter to them do matter to them. Some people may find it uninteresting or even unpleasant to engage in this sort of pretense. Yet although some people have an aversion to playing games, many people find it enjoyable to do so, and this suggests that, for some, it can be pleasurable to inhabit an artificial context of value or importance precisely because of its artificiality. The pressure to do things that really matter, with all the attendant difficulty, risk of failure, and uncertainty involved, can be burdensome. The stakes are high and the difficulties considerable. It can come as a relief to retreat into an artificial, rule-governed world in which, on the one hand, it is very clear what matters and, on the other hand, it is also clear that what matters in the game doesn't really matter. To put the point perhaps too crudely, it can come as a relief to pretend that things matter when they don't.

It seems evident—indeed, it seems like a comical understatement to assert—that the things that matter to us in the context of a game are not dependent for their perceived significance on our confidence in the existence of the afterlife. To the extent that it matters to me in a game of Monopoly to put hotels on my properties, the news that the human race will soon die out does not seem to render that ambition pointless. In the relevant sense, it was already pointless. This marks an obvious contrast with the cases of relief from severe pain and the existence of the afterlife itself, both of which were also said to be examples of things whose importance to us is independent of our confidence that there will be an afterlife. In those cases, the independence seems to be a mark of how much the things in question matter to us, or of the way in which they matter to us, whereas in the case of games, it is a mark of how little they really matter to us.

Does this mean that in the infertility scenario people who had previously enjoyed playing games would continue to do so? Perhaps. That is what we might expect if it really is true that the prospective disappearance of the human race would not undermine the importance to players of what happens in games. However, although I do not pretend to know the answer to the question, and hope never to see it put to the test, there are considerations that tend the other way. The fact that, in ordinary circumstances, it can be enjoyable to inhabit artificial contexts of significance may depend on our taking for granted a wider context in which many things really do matter to us. If it is a relief to inhabit the artificial context, that is presumably because we perceive the normal, nonartificial context as having a burdensomely value-laden character. If we could no longer take that character for granted, and if instead our sense of what was really important to us was already under assault from the infertility scenario, then it is at least unclear whether playing games—feigning significance— would continue to be appealing. Would it continue to be a relief to inhabit artificial contexts of significance when the genuine contexts were no longer available to us? Here two thoughts suggest themselves. The first thought is that if the answer to this question is no, then that may be because, although what matters to us within the context of a game is artificial, the fact that playing games itself matters to us is not similarly artificial. Instead, it matters to us because it gives us relief from the burdensome quest for genuine importance, and it is genuinely and nonartificially important to us to get such relief. In other words, the very pointlessness of playing games is the point of them. But this point itself might be dependent on the existence of the afterlife and so it might be undermined by the infertility scenario. It might no longer seem important to us to seek relief from importance, when there was so little importance available in the first place. The second thought is that if the answer to the question is instead yes, then that may be because games would serve a different kind of function for people in the infertile world. Rather than enjoying the relief that artificial contexts of significance provide from the burdensome quest for real significance, people might enjoy the feigned significance of games because there was so little of genuine significance to be found, and feigned significance turned out to provide an acceptable simulacrum. In much the same way, P. D. James imagines the people in her infertile world lavishing attention on dolls and pets because there are no longer any human babies available.

2.

The next topic I want to address has to do with the limits of our individualism. This is related to the point about the limits of egoism that I have already discussed, but it is nevertheless distinct. The point about egoism had to do with the relative psychological power of our self-interested concerns in comparison with other sorts of motives and attitudes. In speaking now about the limits of individualism, I am interested instead in what the afterlife conjecture reveals about the extent to which individual valuing is, as a conceptual matter, part of a social or collective enterprise or practice. We all know that individuals differ in what they value and what is important to them. The distinctiveness of individuals is partly constituted by the distinctiveness of their personal values and commitments. Moreover, while some individuals have values and commitments with a strong and explicit social orientation, other people do not. They value more solitary pursuits and are less moved either to enter into collaborative ventures or to seek out projects whose explicit purpose is to make some kind of contribution to society. Notwithstanding these variations, however, the afterlife conjecture strongly suggests that much individual valuing, whether or not it has overtly social content or an overtly social orientation, nevertheless has at least an implicit social or collective dimension.

More generally, the entire range of phenomena that consists in people's valuing things, in things mattering or being important to them, or in their caring deeply about them, occurs within the implicit framework of a set of assumptions that includes, at the most basic level, the assumption that human life itself matters, and that it is an ongoing phenomenon with a history that transcends the history of any individual. Our concerns and commitments, our values and judgments of importance, our sense of what matters and what is worth doing—all these things are formed and sustained against a background in which it is taken for granted that human life is itself a thriving, ongoing enterprise. Many of our deepest and most defining values and aspirations and ambitions, for all their felt urgency and for all their associated aura of ultimate or bedrock importance, nevertheless depend on our taking this for granted. In fact, we take it so much for granted that we seldom recognize its role, let alone make it the explicit object of reflection. But this does nothing to diminish its significance. Humanity itself as an ongoing, historical project provides the implicit frame of reference for most of our judgments about what matters. Remove that frame of reference, and our sense of importance—however individualistic it may be in its overt content—is destabilized and begins to erode. We need humanity to have a future if many of our own individual purposes are to matter to us now. Indeed, I believe that something stronger is true: we need humanity to have a future for the very idea that things *matter* to retain a secure place in our conceptual repertoire.

3.

The third topic I want to address concerns the relation between value and temporality. I have already called attention to the conservative aspect of valuing, to the fact that there is something approaching a conceptual connection between valuing something and seeing reasons to preserve or sustain it over time. Perhaps there are cases in which someone genuinely values a thing but is indifferent to whether it survives past the moment, but if so these must surely be very special cases. So this is one respect in which valuing has a temporal dimension: to value X is normally to see reasons for trying to preserve or extend X over time. The fact that what matters to us implicitly depends on our confidence in the existence of an afterlife constitutes a second connection between value and temporality: what matters to us now depends on what we think will happen later. Underlying both of these points, however, is a more general one. Valuing is a diachronic phenomenon in the sense that, in valuing something, one does not merely manifest an occurrent preference about how things go in the future. Instead, one acquires a *stake in* how things go, in whether what one values is realized or achieved or sustained. This is partly a consequence of the fact that valuing any X involves seeing oneself as having X-related reasons for action that extend over time and whose content depends on how X itself fares. And it is partly a consequence of the fact that valuing a thing also involves being emotionally vulnerable to how X fares. When we value something, then, we project ourselves into the future and invest ourselves in that future. Our emotions and our future courses of action both hang in the balance; they both depend on the fate of what we value. In this respect, valuing is both risky and proprietary. It is risky because, in valuing, we give hostages to fortune. If we valued nothing, then the prospect of postmortem asteroids or global infertility would lack the power to disturb us in the way that they do. And it is proprietary because, in valuing, we lay claim to the future—we arrogate to ourselves the authority to make judgments about how the future *should* unfold. In a sense, valuing is a way of trying to control time. It is an attempt to impose a set of standards on time and to make it answerable to us. To value something is to resist the transitoriness of time; it is to insist that the passage of time lacks normative authority. Things may come and things may go, but *we* decide what matters. *Man* is the measure of all things; Protagoras's dictum, understood in this way, sounds a defiant, even hubristic note. Time does not have the last word; it does not tell us what is important.

The fact that valuing is a diachronic phenomenon also enables it to play a stabilizing role in our lives. Our values express our own understanding of ourselves as temporally extended creatures with commitments that endure through the flux of daily experience. Our ordinary desires may and often do persist over time, even over very long periods of time. But to be committed to the persistence of our values is part of what it is for them to be our values (although, needless to say, they may change anyway). And a life lived without any values whatsoever would scarcely be recognizable as a human life at all. It would be more like the life of what Harry Frankfurt calls a "wanton." A wanton, according to Frankfurt, is an agent who is not a person because his actions simply "reflect the economy of his first-order desires," and because he is indifferent to "the enterprise of evaluating" those desires.[1]

4.

Before moving on to my next topic, I want to take a brief detour to discuss the views of Alvy Singer. Alvy Singer, as you may remember, is the character played by Woody Allen in his movie *Annie Hall*. The movie contains a flashback scene in which the nine-year-old Alvy is taken by his mother to see a doctor. Alvy is refusing to do his homework on the ground that the universe is expanding. He explains that "the universe is everything, and if it's expanding, someday it will break apart and that would be the end of everything!"[2] Leaving aside Alvy's nerdy precocity, the scene is funny because the eventual end of the universe is so temporally remote—it won't happen for "billions of years," the doctor assures Alvy—that it seems comical to cite it as a reason for not doing one's homework. But if the universe were going to end soon after the end of his own natural life, then the arguments I have been rehearsing imply that Alvy might have a point. It might well be a serious question whether he still had reason to do his homework. Why should there be this discrepancy? If the end of human life in the near term would make many things matter less to us now, then why aren't we similarly affected by the knowledge that human life will end in the

---

1. See Harry Frankfurt, "Freedom of the Will and the Concept of a Person," *Journal of Philosophy* 68 (1971): 5–20; at 12; at 13.

2. *Annie Hall*, screenplay by Woody Allen and Marshall Brickman, available online at http://www.dailyscript.com/scripts/annie_hall.html.

longer term? The nagging sense that perhaps we should be is also part of what makes Alvy's refusal to do his homework funny.

Yet I take it as a datum that, in general, and allowing for occasional episodes of Alvy-like angst, we are not so affected. We do not feel or behave as we would, for example, in the infertile world. What we require to maintain our equanimity, it seems, is not that humanity should be immortal, but merely that it should survive for a healthy and indefinitely long period after our own deaths. I don't think that we would object to immortality—even Bernard Williams, who thought that personal immortality would be tedious, made no such claim about the immortality of the species[3]—but we don't insist on it. I'm not sure that we can be said exactly to have a *reason* for this, though I'm open to suggestions. My speculation instead is that we simply don't know how, in these contexts, to work

---

3. See Bernard Williams, "The Makropulos Case: Reflections on the Tedium of Immortality," in *Problems of the Self* (Cambridge: Cambridge University Press, 1973), 82–100. Nor, incidentally, is such a claim attributable to Leoš Janáček, whose opera *The Makropulos Case* was one of the inspirations for Williams's article. This much seems clear, for example, from the final scene ("The Forester's Farewell") of another Janáček opera, *The Cunning Little Vixen*—a scene that was performed at the composer's funeral and which Williams himself greatly admired. (An English translation of the libretto for that opera can be found in Timothy Cheek, *The Janáček Opera Libretti: Volume I* [Lanham, MD: The Scarecrow Press, 2003], 172–81. Williams mentions the final scene in "Janáček's Modernism: Doing More with Less in Music and Philosophy," which is included in his *On Opera* [New Haven: Yale University Press, 2006], 118–20.)

In "On Becoming Extinct" (*Pacific Philosophical Quarterly* 83 [2002]: 253–69), James Lenman argues that given that human beings will someday become extinct, it makes no difference from an impersonal perspective whether this happens sooner or later. However, he also holds that we have good (although defeasible) "generation-centred reasons" for preferring that it happen later rather than sooner. And he does not argue for the desirability of human extinction from either the impersonal or the "generation-centred" perspective.

with or even fully to grasp concepts like "the end of the universe" or "billions of years." Those ideas require us to adopt a conceptual and spatiotemporal perspective whose vast scale is difficult to align with the much more restricted frame of reference relative to which we make judgments of significance in our daily lives. The result is that we are simply confounded when we try to integrate such ideas into our thinking about what matters. It's not so much that we are not troubled, or cannot be talked into being troubled, about what will happen in the extremely remote future, it's just that we don't really know how to think about it at all, in part because there are so few contexts in which we have occasion to do so.

5.

I have, by stipulation, been using the term "afterlife" to refer to the continued existence of other people after one's own death. I want now to consider the relation between the afterlife in my sense and the afterlife as it is more commonly understood. Apart from my insistence on using the same word in both cases, and apart from the fact that both ideas involve the continued existence of *someone* after one's death, are there any interesting connections between the two notions? In discussing this question, I will, for the sake of convenience, sometimes refer to the afterlife as it is traditionally understood as "the personal afterlife" and the afterlife in my nonstandard sense as "the collective afterlife." These bits of usage are also stipulative.

One way to begin is by considering the relationship between the ways in which the collective afterlife matters to people and the ways in which the personal afterlife matters to people. It is clear that most people who believe in the existence of the afterlife as it is commonly understood—in the personal afterlife—attach great importance to it. What features are responsible for its perceived importance? There is no simple answer to this question, in part because the idea of "the afterlife as commonly understood" is an oversimplification. Many religious and philosophical traditions have developed conceptions of the personal afterlife, and these conceptions differ from one another in significant respects. I have no hope of doing justice here either to the complexity of these various doctrines or to the differences among them. For my purposes, it will suffice to single out a few prominent features that have often been associated with ideas of the personal afterlife and to which many people have attached a great deal of importance.

The most obvious reason why the afterlife has mattered to people, and the one that I shall therefore say the least about, lies simply in the prospect of personal survival itself. Although I have argued that there are some significant respects in which the survival of others matters more to us than our own survival, it is nevertheless clear that the desire for personal survival is, for many people, an extremely powerful one. Some philosophers, such as Williams, have argued that immortality would not be desirable,[4] and other philosophers have argued that death is neither to be regarded as a misfortune nor to be feared,[5] but it seems safe to say that many people remain unconvinced. As I have emphasized and as is in any case evident, many people find the prospect of death terrifying and are eager to prolong their lives for as long as possible.[6] If the prospect of a

---

4. See Williams, "The Makropulos Case," in *Problems of the Self.* For extended discussion of Williams's position, see Lecture 3.

5. The most famous examples are Epicurus, in his *Letter to Menoeceus*, and Lucretius, in *De Rerum Natura*. For a contemporary defense of the Epicurean position, see Stephen E. Rosenbaum, "How to Be Dead and Not Care: A Defense of Epicurus," *American Philosophical Quarterly* 23 (1986): 217–25. I discuss the reasonableness of fearing death in Lecture 3.

6. Miguel de Unamuno, in a chapter titled "The Hunger for Immortality," gives memorable expression to these attitudes:

> I am presented with arguments...to prove the absurdity of a belief in the immortality of the soul. But these ratiocinations do not move me, for they are reasons and no more than reasons, and one does not feed the

personal afterlife offered nothing more than relief from the fear of death and the prospect of personal survival, it would still be, for many people, overwhelmingly desirable. Without underestimating the appeal of these factors, however, it is important to recognize that the afterlife has mattered to people for other reasons as well.

One very important reason is that it has been regarded as an opportunity to be reunited with loved ones: both with those who died while one was still alive and with those who remained alive after one died. I take it that the desire for this kind of reunion is, along with the desire to avoid death itself, one of the most powerful unsatisfiable desires that human beings have. Even the less ambitious desire simply to be able to communicate with those who have died can be almost unbearably intense. If you have ever had occasion to read the *New York Times*'s death notices, you may have seen the brief "In Memoriam" section at the end, in which people address messages directly to deceased loved ones, usually on their birthdays or on the anniversaries of their deaths. Although I completely understand the desire to communicate with those who have departed, I was for some time puzzled by people's confidence that their loved ones continued to read the *New York Times*. On reflection, however, it has come to seem to me that the impulse to broadcast these sometimes painfully intimate messages in a public forum is actually a rather ingenious way of trying to subvert the impossibility of successful communication with the dead. Roughly speaking, the

heart with reasons. I do not want to die. No! I do not want to die, and I do not want to want to die. I want to live always, forever and ever. And *I* want to live, this poor I which I am, the I which I feel myself to be here and now, and for that reason I am tormented by the problem of the duration of my soul, of my own soul.

I am the center of my Universe, the center of the Universe, and in my extreme anguish I cry, along with Michelet, "My I! They are stealing my I!"

In *The Tragic Sense of Life*, translated by Anthony Kerrigan, edited and annotated by Martin Nozick and Anthony Kerrigan (Princeton, NJ: Princeton University Press, 1972), 51.

publicity masks the impossibility, although why exactly this should be so is a fascinating question that would repay further investigation. To pursue the matter further here, however, would lead us too far astray, and so I will content myself with simply citing this phenomenon as evidence of the intensity with which people long to communicate or to be reunited with the dead. It is clear that one reason why the personal afterlife matters so much to people is that it offers the prospect of satisfying this longing.

A third reason—or set of reasons—has to do with ideas of redemption, vindication, and justice. The personal afterlife as it has traditionally been conceived offers the prospect that the worst deficiencies of this world will somehow be made good in the next. Those who have prospered by treating others cruelly or unjustly will be held to account. Those who have been victimized or oppressed will receive recognition, reward, or recompense. Those who have endured pain, poverty, and loss will at last be granted comfort and relief. The sufferings of the innocent and the triumphs of the vicious, so hard to endure or to accept in this world, will be set in a wider context that makes sense of them and reveals them to have served some purpose that redeems them. They will be explained in ways that we will be able to understand and accept. We will at last be able to see why these things happened, and the explanation will prove satisfying; it will put us in a position to reconcile ourselves to the intolerable cruelties of life on earth. In short, the manifest injustices of this world will be superseded by the cosmic justice of the next. The incomprehensible unfairness of life as we know it will turn out not to have been the final word in human affairs. We will get what we all want: some answers, and some justice. And apart from the desire for personal survival and the desire to be reunited with loved ones, these are perhaps the most powerful human longings to which traditional ideas of the afterlife have spoken: the longing for understanding and the longing for justice.

This leads more or less directly to a fourth reason why the personal afterlife has seemed important to people. If there is no afterlife, and if the injustices of this world are indeed the final word in human affairs, then our worldly lives may seem devoid of purpose, and nothing at all may seem ultimately to matter. Nothing will ever redeem the sufferings of the innocent or undo the triumphs of the wicked. The universe does not care whether the innocent suffer or the wicked prosper, because the universe doesn't care about anything. And if the universe doesn't care then our own caring may seem pointless, because the fact that the universe doesn't care means that nothing really matters in the end. There is no cosmic ledger in which scores are kept and eventually settled. Things just happen, and then they stop happening. There is no cosmic justice, there is no cosmic purpose, and there is nothing at all that ultimately matters. So it really doesn't matter what we do now. We may be kind or cruel, wise or foolish, brilliantly successful or dismally unsuccessful, but it really doesn't matter. None of it is of any ultimate importance, because the idea that anything at all is of ultimate importance is just an illusion. Or, at any rate, that is the nihilistic conclusion that some people have thought we would have to draw if there were no personal afterlife. To these people, it has seemed essential that there should be an afterlife if our worldly lives are to have the kind of purpose or point that would vindicate our ordinary human concerns and aspirations. So understood, the personal afterlife speaks to the deep human desire that our worldly existence should have some ultimate meaning or purpose or significance.

In summary, then, the personal afterlife has seemed important to people for (at least) the following reasons. It has seemed to offer them the prospect of personal survival, of relief from the fear of death, of being reunited with their loved ones, of seeing cosmic justice done, of receiving a satisfying explanation for some of life's most troubling features, and of gaining assurance that their lives have some larger purpose or significance. Now if you are a suspicious person, you may at this point have begun to wonder whether I am going to try to pull a cosmic rabbit out of my humble, professorial hat, and to demonstrate that the collective afterlife can actually deliver on suitably reinterpreted versions of all of these promises. Alas, no such wizardry is in the offing. As far as I can see, no amount of reinterpretive gymnastics will yield any interesting sense in which the fact that others will live on after we have died means that we ourselves can reasonably hope for personal survival after death, or for communication or reunion with our loved ones, or for cosmic justice, or for a satisfying explanation of why the innocent suffer and the wicked prosper. The question of whether the existence of the collective afterlife can vindicate our worldly concerns and help to stave off nihilism is obviously more complicated. It is, in effect, one of the main issues I have been discussing in these lectures, and I will return to it in a moment, but even an affirmative answer would not mean that our lives have some larger cosmic purpose or significance, at least so far as I understand those notions.

My primary interest, however, is not in whether our hopes for the afterlife can be satisfied, but rather in what those hopes and desires can teach us about ourselves and our values. And here I think that, up to a point, a comparison of people's attitudes toward the personal afterlife and their attitudes toward the collective afterlife reveals some interesting common ground. One thing that is striking about the reasons why people have attached importance to the personal afterlife is that those reasons have some of the same nonegoistic and nonindividualistic character that we noted earlier in discussing our attitudes toward the collective afterlife. This is all the more noteworthy because we might naturally have been inclined to assume that, in view of the importance that people attach to personal survival and relief from the fear of death, the afterlife matters to them exclusively because of what it seems to offer on these fronts. However, while these things certainly do matter to people, the considerations I have canvassed suggest another side to the story.

They suggest that people's attitudes toward the personal afterlife also reflect, among other things, two particularly profound desires. The first is the desire to be able to preserve or reclaim one's place in a web of valued social relationships. The second is the desire to be able to live in a just and orderly world, one in which the values of justice and fairness prevail. To the extent that they reflect these desires, people's attitudes toward the personal afterlife reinforce a conclusion that we drew when considering our attitudes toward the collective afterlife: namely, that as much as we may wish for personal survival, we also wish for the survival and flourishing of our social world. Indeed, as they manifest themselves in this case, these two wishes are not sharply separable, for even when people's fantasies of the personal afterlife focus primarily on their own survival and flourishing, they do not normally imagine that they will flourish while living in isolation from the people they care about. On the contrary, they imagine that their relationships with those people will be restored and extended, and it is not clear how much appeal the prospect of a completely solitary afterlife would have for them. Nor do they suppose that their own eternal flourishing will be a piece of exceptional good fortune, and that, in general, the next world will be just as full of cruelty and unfairness as this one. Instead, they implicitly take their own eternal flourishing to consist in living among those they love as part of a just and fair order. And the fact that that is their fantasy of the next world tells us something about what matters to them in this one. It also confirms the nonindividualistic character of human valuing, and shows that the limits of individualism apply not only to those who do not believe in the personal afterlife but also to those who do.

Yet when thinking about the relation between people's attitudes toward the personal afterlife and their attitudes toward the collective afterlife, the most interesting comparison concerns the role of each in underwriting the purpose or significance of our ordinary, worldly lives. As I said, it has seemed to many people as if, in the absence of a personal afterlife, nothing would ultimately matter, and so it would not matter what we do now. Our lives would be devoid of meaning or purpose. Similarly, in discussing the collective afterlife, we noted that if we became convinced that human beings would soon disappear from the earth, then many of the things that now matter to us would seem to us to matter less or not to matter at all. This suggests another point of common ground in our attitudes toward the personal and collective afterlives. Notwithstanding this common ground, however, I believe that there are important and revealing differences between the two sets of attitudes. Although many people sincerely believe that life would lose its purpose and that our ordinary concerns would cease to matter in the absence of a personal afterlife, the evidence nevertheless suggests that most people who do not believe in a personal afterlife are able to carry on quite nicely.

In other words, there are many people who do not believe in the existence of a personal afterlife but for whom the full range of human activities, projects, and relationships continues to matter greatly. Their lack of confidence in the existence of a personal afterlife does not in any way diminish their tendency to invest activities and events with significance. They continue to regard projects and pursuits of many different kinds as valuable and to see themselves as having compelling reasons to undertake those projects and engage in those pursuits. They seek out and become involved in personal relationships that they value deeply, and they recognize and act on the distinctive reasons that arise in the context of such relationships. In pursuing their projects and relationships, moreover, they routinely place themselves in positions where they are vulnerable to a wide range of emotions depending on how those projects and relationships fare. In short, they do not behave like people to whom little or nothing matters or has any importance. Despite their complete lack of conviction about the existence of a personal afterlife, they continue to lead value-laden lives: lives structured by wholehearted engagement in a full array of valued activities and interactions with others.

All this stands in marked contrast to our speculations about how people would behave when faced with a loss of confidence in the collective afterlife. Our primary conjecture about the infertility scenario was that in an infertile world, people would cease to believe in the value of many sorts of activities that they had previously regarded as worthwhile. In addition, they would cease to see themselves as having reason to engage in many familiar sorts of pursuits that they had previously treated as reason-giving. And activities that they had previously engaged in eagerly and whole-heartedly would now elicit a measure of apathy or indifference. In view of these doxastic, deliberative, and emotional changes, people's ability to lead value-laden lives would be seriously eroded.

If these speculations are even roughly accurate, they point to a dramatic conclusion. Although one of the primary reasons why the personal afterlife matters to people is that it offers the prospect of personal survival, and although many people desperately wish to survive for as long as possible, a failure to believe in the existence of the personal afterlife is actually much less likely to erode people's confidence in the value or importance of their worldly pursuits than is a failure to believe in the existence of the collective afterlife, which offers no prospect of personal survival. It is much less likely to lead people to think, to reason, to feel, and to act as if little or nothing was important to them. In these concrete respects, the collective afterlife matters more to people than the personal afterlife. In other words, our confidence that there will be a collective afterlife is, to a much greater extent than our confidence that there will be a personal afterlife, a condition of other things mattering to us here and now.

So we have arrived at the same conclusion that we reached in Lecture 1 from a different starting point. In some very basic respects, our own survival, and even the survival of those we love and care about most deeply, matters less to us than the survival of strangers, the survival of humanity itself. Just to be clear, let me distinguish this conclusion from some other conclusions about survival that philosophers have drawn. Some philosophers have argued that even if we reject traditional conceptions of the personal afterlife, there is nevertheless an important sense in which at least some of us *can* hope to survive our own deaths, so the personal afterlife, understood in a certain way, is not entirely out of reach.[7] Other philosophers have argued not that there is a personal afterlife, but rather that if we understood what personal survival consists in, then it might come to matter to us less than it does, and the survival of others might come to matter to us more.[8] By contrast, my argument has been that personal survival already *does* matter to us less than we tend to suppose, and that the survival of humanity matters to us more. In saying this, I am not underestimating our powerful impulses to personal survival or the deep terror that many people feel when contemplating their own deaths. Nor am I denying the importance of self-interested motivations in ordinary human behavior. My point is that despite the power of these attitudes, there is a very specific sense in which our own survival is less important to us than the survival of the human race. The prospect of the imminent disappearance of the race poses a far greater threat to our ability to treat other things as mattering to us and, in so doing, it poses a far greater threat to our continued ability to lead value-laden lives.

6.

One way to challenge this conclusion would be to argue as follows. What has been shown, it might be said, is that for people who do not believe in a personal afterlife, the prospect of the imminent disappearance of the human race poses a greater threat to their ability to lead value-laden lives than does the prospect of their own deaths. But this comparative claim is not true of those who do believe in a

7. See Mark Johnston, *Surviving Death* (Princeton, NJ: Princeton University Press, 2010).

8. See Derek Parfit, *Reasons and Persons* (Oxford: Clarendon Press, 1984), 281–82.

personal afterlife. For them, the prospect of the disappearance of the race would be far less threatening, since they expect to survive their own deaths in any case. What the argument therefore demonstrates is only that in order for one's capacity to lead a value-laden life to be secure, one must believe either in a personal or in a collective afterlife: either in one's own survival after one's death or in the survival of others.

As I said at the beginning of Lecture 1, I am concerned primarily with the attitudes of people who do not believe in the personal afterlife. So the suggestion that the comparative claim applies only to them is not something I am committed to denying. But if indeed the comparative claim holds true only of them, this fact should itself strike us as remarkable. It should strike us as remarkable that people who do *not* believe they will survive their own deaths would nevertheless be more threatened by the prospect of the disappearance of the human race than by the prospect of their own deaths. We might have expected just the reverse to be true. Since these people do not expect to survive their own deaths, and since many of them want desperately to survive, we might have supposed that the prospect of their own deaths would be far more threatening to them than the prospect that humanity as a whole would die out. And we might have supposed that if the comparative claim were true of anyone, it would be true of those who *do* believe in the personal afterlife, and who therefore expect to survive their own deaths. We might have supposed that, because of these beliefs, this group of people would be less threatened by the prospect of their own deaths than by the prospect of the disappearance of humanity.

In fact, as this last point suggests, the question of whether the comparative claim applies to those who do believe in the personal afterlife is more complex than it may seem. After all, these people expect to survive their own deaths, and so, we may assume, the prospect of their own deaths poses no threat at all to their capacity to lead value-laden lives. Relative to that low baseline, the prospect of humanity's disappearance might well pose a greater threat. On the other hand, those who believe in a personal afterlife for themselves normally believe that such an afterlife is available to others as well, so for these believers the end of human life on earth might also seem to pose little threat. In that case, the correct conclusion would be that neither the prospect of their own deaths nor the prospect of humanity's disappearance would pose much of a threat to their ability to lead value-laden lives. Yet this is a bit too quick, since the imminent disappearance of human life on earth would presumably lead even these believers to lose interest in a wide-range of future-oriented projects, such as the project of finding a cure for cancer, which would be rendered pointless under the terms of the infertility scenario. And it is not obvious how far-reaching these effects would be.

Still, it may be correct to assert, as the challenge we are considering does, that in order for one's capacity to lead a value-laden life to be secure, one must believe in one form of afterlife or the other. One must believe either in the personal afterlife or in the collective afterlife. This claim, if true, is certainly significant. But it is significant for three reasons, all of which are congenial to the position I have been developing. First, it calls attention to one of the potential dangers of a belief in the personal afterlife, namely, that such a belief may reconcile people too readily to the disappearance of life on earth, and make it seem less urgent to prevent this from happening. Second, it reinforces the point made earlier about the limits of individualism. That is, it confirms the dependence of human valuing on our confidence that humanity has a future: whether that future is of the conventional kind represented by the collective afterlife or the very different kind represented by the personal afterlife. Finally, it emphasizes once again the unexpected character of the attitudes I have described. It is not, perhaps, surprising that a belief in the personal afterlife should protect the believers' ability to lead value-laden lives in this world. What *is* surprising is that, for the rest of us, our ability to lead such lives would be more threatened by the prospect of humanity's disappearance than by the prospect of our own deaths, despite the fact that we neither want to die nor expect to survive our deaths.

Of course, the very fact that this conclusion is surprising may seem like a reason for doubting its truth. If it really were true that we were less concerned with our own survival than with the survival of humanity as a whole, how could we possibly be unaware of this? In addressing this question, it is important to keep in mind the limited scope of the conclusion I have drawn. I have not claimed that we are in general or in all contexts less concerned with our own survival than with the survival of humanity. What I have said is only that there is one important respect in which this is so. The point, again, is that our continuing to regard things as mattering to us in our worldly lives is more dependent on our confidence in the survival of humanity than it is on our confidence in our own survival.

If this comes as a surprise to us, that is partly because we generally take the collective afterlife for granted. This means that, fiction and philosophy aside, we never have occasion to experience or to confront the reactions we would have if the destruction of humanity were imminent. So the importance to us of the collective afterlife is masked or hidden from view. We don't recognize how much it matters to us. By contrast, we know perfectly well that we will die, and we are intimately acquainted with our reactions to that fact. Given the power of these reactions and the central role that our attitudes toward our own deaths play in our lives, it seems preposterous to claim that we are actually more concerned about the survival of humanity than we are about our own survival. But that is because we are making the wrong comparison. We are comparing our reactions to our own imminent annihilation, which we fully expect to happen, with our reactions to the survival of the human race, which we generally take for granted. However, the relevant comparison is between our actual reactions to our own imminent annihilation and the reactions we would have to the imminent annihilation of the human race, if we were as confident that it was about to occur as we are of our own deaths. And my claim is that, despite the dread and terror with which many people face the prospect of their own deaths, there is one extremely important respect in which many face that prospect with greater equanimity than they would exhibit if faced with the imminent disappearance of humanity itself. Things continue to matter to them even though they know they will die, and the prospect of their deaths does not exert the same depressive effect on their ability to live value-laden lives as would the prospective disappearance of humanity itself.

Despite what I have said, this may continue to seem surprising. If so, that is partly because we tend to believe our own bad press and to overestimate the extent of our egoism. As I argued earlier, the fact that, in certain respects, we care less about our own survival than about the survival of humanity shows something important and insufficiently appreciated about the limits of our egoism. In part, our surprise when this is pointed out simply confirms the insufficiency of our appreciation. However, there is a distinction that needs to be drawn here. The assertion that we care less about own survival than about the survival of humanity might be understood in two different ways. It might be taken to mean that we are less motivated to ensure our own survival than we are to ensure the survival of humanity. Or it might mean that we are more dependent for our equanimity on our confidence in the survival of humanity than on our confidence in our own survival. Although references to the limits of our egoism might suggest the first interpretation, it is the second interpretation that is supported by the arguments I have offered. The point has not been that we are more highly motivated to advance the interests of future generations, but rather that we are in certain ways more dependent on them. If we find this surprising, it is less because we have been blinded to our own altruism than because we have overestimated our independence and self-sufficiency. In one way, of course, it is no news that death marks the limits of our self-sufficiency. Death amounts to personal annihilation, and there is nothing we can do to avoid it no matter how much we want to and no matter how hard we try. But the considerations I have been rehearsing suggest a different kind of limit to our self-sufficiency. They reveal that we are vulnerable to catastrophe befalling the rest of humanity in a way that we are not vulnerable to our own deaths. And it is the extent of our vulnerability to others that we may find surprising, that may bring us up short.

Of course, if our vulnerability is as great as I have said it is, then perhaps we should be more highly motivated than we are to help ensure that humanity survives. We should be less egoistic in that sense too. The reasons that we have for attending to the interests of future generations are often conceptualized as obligations of justice or seen as grounded in our responsibilities to our descendants. This discourse of obligation and responsibility reinforces our tendency to think that the salient features of our relations to future generations are our power over them and their dependence on us. And it represents the reasons we have for taking their interests into account as moral reasons which should override our concern for ourselves. But the considerations I have been advancing suggest that we also have reasons of a very different kind for attending to the interests of future generations, and that is simply because they matter so much to us. In certain respects, their survival matters more to us than our own. From this perspective, what is salient is not their dependence on us but rather our dependence on them. This is not to deny that they *are* causally dependent on us in obvious ways. But from the perspective I have sketched, their causal dependence on us, rather than being a source of burdensome obligations, provides us instead with welcome opportunities, for to the extent that the collective afterlife matters to us more than the personal afterlife, it is a stroke of good fortune that it is also more under our control. There are actually things we can do to promote the survival and flourishing of humanity after our deaths, such as taking action to solve the problems of climate change and nuclear proliferation, for example. By contrast, there is nothing at all that we can do to promote our own personal survival after our deaths. So perhaps if we recognize the extent of our dependence on future generations, then that will strengthen our determination to act in their behalf, and make us less egoistic in that sense too.

Having said this, however, I must now add that I think that the dichotomy I have drawn between two different ways in which we might be said to care more about the survival of humanity than about our own survival is too simple. It is too simple to say that we care more only in the sense that we are more dependent on the survival of humanity and not in the sense that we are more highly motivated to help ensure it. I think there are at least some contexts in which we would also be more highly motivated to ensure the survival of humanity than we would be to ensure our own survival. Imagine, for example, that you are presented with a choice between two options. If you choose Option 1 rather than Option 2, then you will die sooner, but humanity will survive long after you are dead. If you choose Option 2 rather than Option 1, then you will live longer, but the rest of humanity will immediately perish, and you will live out your remaining years as the only human being on earth. Which would you choose? I think that my own aversion to death is as strong as anyone's, but I would not hesitate to choose the first option, and I suspect that the same is true for many of you. If that is right, then the survival of humanity matters more to us than our own survival not merely in the sense that we are in certain ways more dependent on it, but also in the sense that we would in certain contexts be more highly motivated to bring it about.

At least in my own case, however, it would be misleading to interpret these preferences as evidence of hitherto unsuspected reserves of altruism. To the extent that my reasons for preferring the first option to the second go beyond my recognition of the ways in which what matters to me now depends on the survival of others after my death, those reasons stem primarily from a conviction that to live in a world without other people would be to live in a world without value, a world in which nothing, or almost nothing, mattered. In fact, I would choose not to live on as the only human being on earth even if the alternative were not that human society would survive after my death but rather that everyone including me would die. What is most salient about this preference is what it reveals not about the limits of our egoism but about the equally unappreciated limits of our individualism. In other words, it reflects the strongly social character of human valuing: the extent to which the assumption of an ongoing social life is an implicit precondition of our ability to lead what I have called value-laden lives. To the extent that we would prefer to die rather than to live on alone, what that tells us is that we do not see much prospect of living a worthwhile life in a world otherwise uninhabited by human beings.[9]

7.

Life is too short, but these two lectures have gone on long enough. Let me bring them to a close by providing a brief summary of my main contentions. I have argued that the survival of people after our deaths matters greatly to us, both in its own right and because it is a condition of many other things that now matter to us continuing to do so. In some very significant respects, we actually care more about the survival of others after our deaths than we do about the existence of a personal afterlife, and the imminent disappearance of the human race would have a more corrosive effect on our ability to lead what I have called "value-laden lives" than does the

---

9. But consider, instead of the choice described in the text, the following variant, which was suggested to me by Niko Kolodny. If you choose Option 1, then once again you will die sooner, but humanity will survive long after you are dead. If you choose Option 2, however, then you will live to a ripe old age, but humanity will perish when you do. If you would choose Option 1 under these conditions, that cannot be because of an unwillingness to live as the only human being on earth.

actual prospect of our own deaths. These facts teach us something both about the limits of our egoism and about the limits of our individualism. They also help to illuminate some general features of human valuing. They highlight its conservative, nonexperiential, and nonconsequentialist dimensions. In addition, they shed light on the complex relations between value and temporality. Valuing is itself a diachronic or temporally extended phenomenon, and it is also one of the ways in which we try to exert some kind of control over time, to make time answerable to us rather than the reverse. Not surprisingly, time also figures more directly, and in more than one way, in our reactions to the afterlife scenarios that I discussed. Among other things, those reactions provide evidence of our desire to establish a personalized relation to the future in the face of our certain deaths, and one of the reasons why the survival of others after our deaths matters so much to us is that it is required if we are to succeed in doing this. Indeed, one of the reasons why the disappearance of the human race is such a terrible prospect for each of us is that it marks the ultimate defeat of all of our strategies, as individuals and in groups, for mastering time and its terrors. But it is also a terrible prospect because, to an extent that we rarely acknowledge, our conviction that things matter is sustained by our confidence that life will go on after we ourselves are gone. In this respect, as I have argued, the survival of humanity matters more to each of us than we usually realize; indeed, in this respect, it matters more to us even than our own survival.

Lecture 3: Fear, Death, and Confidence

I have said nothing yet about how one should regard the prospect of one's own death. Even if, as I have maintained, there is an important and neglected respect in which the survival of humanity as a whole matters more to us than our own survival, it would be absurd to claim that our own survival does not matter to us at all. Not only is the desire for personal survival an extremely powerful one in most people but, in addition, it is clear that people's awareness of their mortality exerts a profound and pervasive influence on their other attitudes and motives. Yet the question of what attitude one should take toward one's death has been a vexed question since ancient times. I want now to investigate some of the puzzles and perplexities to which this question has given rise. I will assess the reasonableness of various attitudes one may have to the prospect of one's death, and I will consider how those assessments relate to the conclusions reached earlier about the importance to us of the collective afterlife.

What attitude, then, is it reasonable to have toward the prospect of one's own death? When people are suffering greatly they some-times long for death. Under less extreme conditions, many people fear death and some find it terrifying. Others are able to face it with acceptance and equanimity—or so I'm told. Epicurus and Lucretius, whose writings on the subject continue to exert fascination, argued that we have no reason to fear death. In the most famous passage from his writings on the topic Epicurus memorably said: "So death, the most terrifying of ills, is nothing to us, since so long as we exist, death is not with us; but when death comes, then we do not exist. It does not then concern either the living or the dead, since for the former it is not, and the latter are no more."[1]

One immediate objection to the argument of this passage is that it seems to imply not only that we have no reason to fear death but also that nobody can ever have reason to wish for death. Imagine, however, a torture victim who is undergoing such horrible agonies at the hands of a sadistic Epicurean that he begs his tormenter to kill him. And imagine that the Epicurean torturer replies: "So death, the thing you fervently desire, is nothing to you, since so long as you exist, death is not with you; but when death comes, then you will not exist. It does not then concern you either when you are living or when you are dead, since in the first case it is not, and in the second case you are no more." If the Epicurean torturer's response seems preposterous, then it is unclear why Epicurus's own response to those who fear death should be any less so.

Despite this, and despite the fact that, as Fred Feldman has written, "most of us cannot help but view ...[Epicurus's argument] as sophistry,"[2] philosophers have not found it easy to say where exactly the argument goes wrong and many of them still take it as the starting point for their reflections on death. In so doing, however, they have interpreted the conclusion of Epicurus's argument in different ways. For example, many have taken him to be arguing that death is not bad for the person who dies, or, alternatively, that it is not a misfortune for that person or an evil. Let us call this the First Epicurean Conclusion. I began by mentioning a different claim, the claim that one has no reason to fear one's own death. We can call this the Second Epicurean Conclusion. The relation between these two claims is uncertain. Offhand, it is not obvious that a person has

1. Epicurus, *Epistula ad Menoeceum*, in *Epicurus: The Extant Remains*, trans. Cyril Bailey (Oxford: Clarendon Press, 1926), 82–93, at 85.

2. Fred Feldman, "Some Puzzles About the Evil of Death," *The Philosophical Review* 100 (1991): 205–27, at 205.

reason to fear something if and only if that thing is bad for the person.

Yet some philosophers have argued against the First Epicurean Conclusion without making clear how they take their arguments to bear on the Second Epicurean Conclusion. In his influential essay, "Death," for example, Thomas Nagel argues that death can be bad for the person who dies because it deprives him of future goods, including the very general goods of "perception, desire, activity, and thought."[3] This so-called deprivation theory has proven quite popular among philosophers, although of course it has its critics. For my purposes, however, the theory's merits as an account of the badness of death are beside the point. The question that concerns me is what, if anything, the theory tells us about the fear of death. Nagel does not address this question. So it is not clear whether he thinks that his account demonstrates the reasonableness of such fear. That is, it is not clear whether he thinks that the account suffices to rebut the Second Epicurean Conclusion as well as the First. Construed as a response to the Second Epicurean Conclusion, the deprivation theory would presumably hold that it *is* reasonable for a person to fear death because death will deprive the person of future goods. Offhand, this suggestion does not seem altogether satisfying. It is true that a person may fear, as he anticipates his own death, that it will deprive him of some experience or opportunity to which he is especially looking forward: the opportunity to attend a child's wedding, for example, or to witness the birth of a grandchild. But these sorts of anxieties, although common and sometimes intense, do not seem quite to capture the particularly stark form of terror that many people experience when contemplating their deaths.

In some people at least, there is a distinctive kind of terror that is produced by the strange and sui generis character of the thought that I myself—the thinker of my thoughts, the perceiver of what I

3. Thomas Nagel, "Death," in *Mortal Questions* (Cambridge: Cambridge University Press, 1979), 1–10; quote at 2.

perceive—will simply stop being. This is a thought that can in certain moods induce a kind of vertigo; it can seem uncanny, even impossible (as Nagel himself emphasizes in some of his later writings about death[4]). Although I have had the experience before of losing things that mattered to me or of having good things end, it is *I* who have had those experiences. The losses and endings, however painful, have been experienced against the background of my own (perceived) persistence. But I take death to mean that the very *I* that has had those experiences is what is now going to end. The egocentric subject—which is what has provided the fixed background for all my previous endings—is itself to end. My only resources for reacting to this prospect seem to involve turning back on myself a set of attitudes—such as sadness, grief, rage, anxiety—that are tailored to circumstances in which the self endures and undergoes a loss. But those attitudes become unmoored when directed toward their very subject. And this induces, or can induce, *panic*. It can seem completely incomprehensible and terrifying, even impossible. In the words of Philip Larkin:

> This is a special way of being afraid
> No trick dispels . . .[5]

It is at best unclear whether the deprivation theory can, or is intended to, establish the reasonableness of such fear and thus rebut the Second Epicurean Conclusion. As it stands, the theory simply does not engage with the Epicurean claim about the unreasonableness of fearing death. In consequence, it has two serious limitations. It is limited, first, as a response to the Epicurean position, whose ultimate motivation is precisely to relieve people of the fear of death by demonstrating its unreasonableness. The Epicurean

4. See, for example, Thomas Nagel, *The View from Nowhere* (New York: Oxford University Press, 1986), 223–31.

5. From Philip Larkin, *Aubade*, first published in the *Times Literary Supplement*, December 23, 1977.

employs a strategy that might be termed "using metaphysics to fight fear,"[6] and if the deprivation theory ignores that strategy and that ambition then it fails to engage the heart of the Epicurean position. The theory as it stands is also limited as an independent assessment of the significance of death, for surely much of the interest of the question of whether death is an evil lies in its implications for how we should view the prospect of our own deaths. The claim that death is bad for a person, unsupplemented by any claim about what attitudes it is appropriate to have toward this particular bad thing, is bound to strike us as incomplete.

There are of course some theories of value, such as Thomas Scanlon's "buck-passing" account, according to which claims about the goodness or badness of a given object are to be understood as claims to the effect that the object has properties in virtue of which we have reasons to take certain attitudes toward it.[7] On this account, then, the claim that death is bad for a person should be interpreted as the claim that we have reasons to take certain attitudes toward our deaths. This assimilates evaluative claims about the goodness or badness of death to normative claims about the reasonableness of our attitudes toward death. In so doing, it offers a way of interpreting the deprivation theory as making normative claims and not merely evaluative ones. The problem, however, is that the buck-passing account itself does not tell us *which* attitudes toward any particular good or bad object are reasonable. And so even if the deprivation theory is seen through the lens of the buck-passing account, this still does not tell us whether death is something toward which fear in particular is a reasonable attitude.

6. Katja Vogt has pointed out to me that the Epicurean philosophers would not have accepted this description of their aims, since they took themselves to be appealing to physics (or natural science) to fight fear rather than to metaphysics as they understood it.

7. See Thomas Scanlon, *What We Owe to Each Other* (Cambridge, MA: Harvard University Press, 1998).

In his essay on "The Makropulos Case," Bernard Williams joins Nagel in rejecting the First Epicurean Conclusion and arguing that death is normally an evil, although the basis for his position is somewhat different from Nagel's.[8] His essay also has in common with Nagel's a failure to take up questions about the reasonableness of fearing death or to engage with the Second Epicurean Conclusion. Williams does call attention to the distinction between the two Epicurean claims, however, and he explicitly sets aside the question of whether death is to be feared. His main ambition, in addition to establishing that death is normally an evil, is to argue that there is a sense in which it nevertheless gives the meaning to our lives, because an immortal life would be a meaningless one. But although he does not address the question of whether death is to be feared, he does suggest, intriguingly, that his position does not rule this out. Just as, in his view, death can reasonably be regarded as an evil despite the fact that it gives the meaning to life, so too, he suggests but does not argue, it may be that we have reason to fear death despite the fact that it is a condition of the meaningfulness of our lives. I believe that this combination of attitudes is in fact reasonable, and I will say more later about why. But first I want to examine Williams's reasons for the two elements of his own position: the claim that death is an evil and the claim that it gives the meaning to our lives.

Williams's argument that death is an evil turns on his distinction between categorical and conditional desires. Some desires are conditional on continued life: if I continue living, then I want to go to the dentist to have my cavity filled, but I don't want to go on living in order to have my cavity filled. By contrast, if one wants something unconditionally or categorically, then one's desire is not conditional

---

8. Bernard Williams, "The Makropulos Case: Reflections on the Tedium of Immortality," in *Problems of the Self* (Cambridge: Cambridge University Press, 1973), 82–100. Page references for this article will be given parenthetically in the text.

on being alive. Or, as Williams puts it, it does not "hang from the assumption of one's existence" (86). I may, for example, have a categorical desire to finish my novel or to see my children grow up. If so, then I have reasons to resist death, since death would mean that those desires could not be satisfied. And this, Williams thinks, is as much as to say that I have reason to regard death as an evil.

Now it is worth noting that if a categorical desire is taken to be one that could not be satisfied if one died, then the distinction between conditional and categorical desires is not exhaustive. For example, I have a desire that climate change be reversed, and this desire is neither conditional nor categorical in the senses just specified. I do not want climate change to be reversed only on condition that I go on living. But neither do I need to go on living in order for the desire to be fulfilled—climate change could be reversed without me. Williams does not deny the possibility of such desires,[9] but their existence is obscured by his statement that "if I desire something, then, other things being equal, I prefer a state of affairs in which I get it to one in which I do not get it" (85). It is natural to suppose that in order to "get what one wants,"

9. He acknowledges in a footnote that there are some desires that need not go unfulfilled if one dies, and refers to his discussion of "non-I desires" in "Egoism and Altruism" (also included in *Problems of the Self*). He adds that these desires "do not affect the present discussion, which is within the limits of egoistic rationality" (85n). It is unclear whether he considers such desires to be a subset of categorical desires, which he is simply not concerned with in "The Makropulos Case," or whether he means instead to be defining categorical desires as ones that cannot be fulfilled if one dies, so that the desires in question are neither conditional nor categorical. In this lecture, I proceed on the second assumption, largely for convenience, and because Williams himself tends to speak as if categorical desires always give one reasons to resist death. But this is a definitional matter on which nothing of importance rests. It is worth noting, however, that, contrary to what Williams suggests, some of the desires that need not go unfulfilled if one dies seem to fall "within the limits of egoistic rationality." For example, I may want to be considered a great novelist on the strength of the novel I published last year.

one must be alive. But this will be true only for desires that are in a certain way self-referential. If the thing I want is to see my children grow up, then my "getting" that thing consists in my seeing them grow up, and that requires me to be alive. But if the thing I want is for climate change to be reversed, then my "getting" the thing consists in climate change's being reversed, which does not require me to be alive. It is also worth noting that there are some desires that are conditional not on my being alive, as in the case of the desire to have my cavity filled, but rather on my being dead. In other words, they hang from the assumption not of my existence but of my nonexistence. For example, I may want lots of people to attend my funeral or my novel to be read a hundred years after my death. If so, then these are things I want on the assumption that I die; I don't want to die in order that lots of people may attend my funeral or that my novel may be read a hundred years after my death. The nonexhaustiveness of the distinction between conditional and categorical desires will be of some significance later on, but I want to turn now to the second element of Williams's position, namely, his claim that death gives the meaning to our lives.

On the face of it, Williams's account of the evil of death generates a straightforward prima facie argument in favor of immortality. Categorical desires, as he says, *propel one* into the future, and so long as we have categorical desires, we have reason to resist death. If we always have such desires, we always have reason to avoid death, and if we always have reason to avoid death, then it seems that we have reason to want immortality. What makes immortality undesirable despite this, according to Williams, is that it would actually lead to the elimination of categorical desire and the presence of *boredom*. Although, as I have indicated, I am inclined to agree with Williams that immortality would be undesirable, and that there is a sense in which death gives the meaning to life, I don't think my reasons are the same as his. In fact, I'm not sure that I really understand his reasons.

One source of doubt lies in the fact that Williams's organizing example is that of Elina Makropulos, the eponymous character who gives her name to Janáček's opera and to the play by Karel Čapek on which it is based, but who also has a number of other names with the same initials, and who is usually referred to by Williams simply as EM. EM concludes that she has had enough of life, and decides to forego the opportunity for immortality, at the relatively young age of 342, after having remained age 42 for three hundred years (however chronologically incoherent that may sound).[10] It is very unclear whether the considerations that bear on her decision, as Williams interprets them, actually derive from features of immortality per se, or whether they derive instead from features of any excessively long life. Suppose, for example, that the normal life span for human beings was 1,000 years; let's call this a "very long life." Or suppose that it were a million years (a "super-long life"), or a trillion years (an "ultra-long life"). Would the 342-year-old EM have been happy to go on living under these assumptions? If not, if she would still have been determined to draw things to a close, then the boredom or tedium of which Williams speaks is not a distinctive feature or consequence of an immortal existence; it would equally be a feature of any excessively long life, where the standards of excessive length fall well short of immortality.

In fact, EM's predicament, as Williams describes it, seems to be the product of her life experience to that point rather than a problem posed by the prospect of immortality in particular. In that sense, it derives from backward-looking rather than forward-looking features of her situation. Her boredom, by the time she reaches 342, is connected with the fact that "everything that could happen and make sense to one particular human being of 42 had already happened to her" (90). Her character, by the age of 42, was already

10. I will follow Williams in speaking of EM as 342 years old. However, in the versions of the opera and the play with which I am familiar, she is usually said to be 337.

formed and fixed, and it is relative to her fixed character that everything that could happen and make sense to her had already happened to her by age 342. At that point, new experiences cannot really affect her, and she must withdraw from real engagement with the world. As Williams describes it, "her boredom and distance from life both kill [categorical] desire and consist in the death of it" (91). And the death of categorical desire means that she no longer has any reason to go on living.

If EM's problem is as Williams describes it, then it wouldn't help if what she had to look forward to was not immortality—an eternity of being 42—but merely an ultra-long or a super-long or even a very long life. After all, it is not the prospect of remaining eternally 42 that has led to the death of categorical desire in her, but rather the three hundred years she has already spent at that age. Once those three hundred years have elapsed, categorical desire has already vanished, and EM lacks any reason to remain 42 for even a moment longer—let alone for an ultra-long or a super-long or even a very long time.

This might lead one to wonder whether the Makropulos model of immortality, in which one reaches a certain age, such as 42, and then remains that age forever, is the best model to use for Williams's purposes. He does consider one alternative model, in which one's immortal existence is characterized by the living of a series of psychologically disjoint lives. He rejects this model because he thinks it cannot satisfy two conditions that are necessary in order for immortality to be something I might hope for: namely, that the person who survives forever should be *me*, and that the state in which I survive should bear some relation to the aims I now have in wanting to survive. One might try to rebut this objection, or, alternatively, one might argue that there are still other models of immortality that Williams does not consider. But for our purposes, the relevant point is that, if the model of serial, disjoint lives is indeed unsatisfactory, its deficiencies, like those of the Makropulos model, will emerge long before immortality is in question. If, as an alternative to immediate death, I am offered the opportunity to embark on a new, psychologically disjoint life, and if Williams is correct in thinking that this new life would not constitute a form of survival that I had reason to desire, then that fact would not depend on the chain of disjoint lives continuing forever. Instead, the deficiencies of this form of survival would be fully manifest here and now, and they would hardly be diminished if I were told that the series of disjoint lives would eventually end, albeit after a very long time, in ordinary death.

So, as I have said, it is unclear whether Williams's worries are worries about immortality per se or whether they are instead worries about living too long. In fact, there are reasons for thinking that Williams's ultimate concern is with a problem which, if his diagnosis is correct, lies at the heart of ordinary, mortal life. The problem has to do with a certain tension between the possession of a character and the ability to engage with the world. We have already seen that, in EM's case, it is the constancy of her character, which is already in place by the age of 42, that is supposed to limit her ability, once she reaches the age of 342, to sustain categorical desires and to remain engaged with the world around her. And her inability to remain engaged produces the boredom that leads her to opt out of the immortal existence that is available to her. So there is a tension, it seems, between the possession of a character and the ability to take an interest in life. For someone who was immortal, Williams writes, boredom "would be not just a tiresome effect, but a reaction almost perceptual in character to the poverty of one's relation to the environment. Nothing less will do for eternity than something that makes boredom *unthinkable*. What could that be? Something that could be guaranteed to be at every moment utterly absorbing? But if a man has and retains a character, there is no reason to suppose that there is anything that could be that" (95).

One cannot resolve this tension by deciding to abandon constancy of character, for then, Williams suggests, one will lack any basis for confidence that the person who survives and takes an interest in life will be oneself. In response to the suggestion that intellectual activity in particular might be "at every moment totally absorbing" he writes: "but if one is totally and perpetually absorbed in such an activity, and loses oneself in it, then as those words suggest, we come back to the problem of satisfying the conditions that it should be me who lives forever, and that the eternal life should be in prospect of some interest" (96). Although Williams doesn't put it this way, the source of the boredom that ultimately defeats life is *oneself*. In order to have reasons to live, or to care whether one survives, one must have categorical desires. The possession of categorical desires permits participation in absorbing activities and engagement with the world. In so doing, it permits one to lose oneself. However, the possession of a constant character limits the possibilities of absorption; it results eventually in the death of categorical desire and withdrawal from the world. Yet without a constant character, one has no hope of living on as oneself at all. If one does live on as oneself, one must therefore expect that, eventually, categorical desire will die. Then one will be left with nothing *but* oneself, and one will be doomed to a kind of boredom from which there is no escape in this world. As Williams says in the final paragraph of his essay: "Suppose, then, that categorical desire does sustain the desire to live. So long as it remains so, I shall not want to die. Yet I also know, if what has gone before is right, that an eternal life would be unlivable. In part, as EM's case originally suggested, that is because categorical desire would go away from it: in those versions, such as hers, in which I am recognizably myself, I would eventually have had altogether too much of myself" (100).

Although an eternal life would bring this problem to the fore, it is not the ultimate source of the problem. The ultimate problem is deeper, and it is a problem about human life. We want to live our lives and to be engaged with the world around us. Categorical desires give us reasons to live, and they support such engagement. But when we are engaged, and so succeed in leading the kinds of lives we want, then the way we succeed is by losing ourselves in absorbing activities. When categorical desire dies, as it must do eventually if we have sufficient constancy of character to define selves worth wanting to sustain in the first place, then we will be left *with* ourselves, and we ourselves are, terminally, boring. The real problem is that one's reasons to live are, in a sense, reasons not to live as oneself. It is I who wants to live, but I want to live by losing myself—by not being me. That is the paradox or puzzle that, if Williams is correct, lies at the heart of human experience, and rather than being a consequence of immortality, it is always with us mortals. Most people die before it is transformed into the kind of acute practical problem that undoes EM, although some do not and, as I have already emphasized, her problem becomes unbearable at the relatively young age of 342 and results from the excessively long life she has already led rather than from the immortality that is in prospect.

By contrast, I want to consider some difficulties with immortality itself. In other words, I will advance reasons for thinking that we need to die, not because otherwise we would eventually succumb to a problem that is already inherent in the conditions of human life, but rather because an eternal life would, in a sense, be no life at all.[11]

The basic point is simple. Our lives are so pervasively shaped by the understanding of them as temporally limited that to suspend that understanding would call into question the conditions under

11. I am here implicitly assuming that there are only two possibilities: either one actually dies or one necessarily lives forever—that is, one is subject to no risk of death at any time. I shall continue to rely on this oversimplified dichotomy in what follows. But it is worth mentioning some intermediate cases. One is the case in which, although one does live forever, this is a contingent fact: death is a real possibility at each moment. Another, suggested by the Makropulos example, is the case in which one lives forever provided that one reaffirms one's wish to do so at periodic intervals. Even if one accepts the general thrust of my arguments, these cases raise the question of whether what we really need is actually to die or only to be subject to the possibility of death.

which we value our lives and long for their extension.[12] Consider, for example, the fact that we understand a human life as having stages, beginning with birth and ending with death, and that we understand each of these stages as having its characteristic tasks, challenges, and potential rewards. Although the individuation of stages is culturally variable and although changes in the circumstances of human life may actually result in the emergence of new stages, the fact that life is understood as having stages is, I take it, a universal response to the realities of our organic existence and our physical birth, maturation, deterioration, and death. Our collective understanding of the range of goals, activities, and pursuits that are available to a person, the challenges he faces, and the satisfactions that he may reasonably hope for are all indexed to these stages. The very fact that the accomplishments and the satisfactions of each stage count as *accomplishments and satisfactions* depends on their association with the stage in question: on how much time is taken to be available for the stage; on its place in the succession of stages; and on the physical, mental, and social capacities of a human being at that stage. We do not think that the joys and accomplishments of a mature adult are available to or appropriate for a child or those of an adolescent for an elderly person. We would not think as we do about the joys or the perils of childhood, or of mature adulthood, or of old age, if we did not implicitly see those stages as part of a progression of stages, each with its own expected duration and relations to the other stages.

Consider, too, the role played in human life, and in our understanding of human life, by such things as loss, illness, injury, harm, risk, and danger. Consider how much effort we expend in trying to

12. In developing this point, I have benefited from an unpublished paper by Katja Vogt and from conversations with Nathana O'Brien. A similar argument is developed by Martha Nussbaum in *The Therapy of Desire* (Princeton, NJ: Princeton University Press, 1994), 225–32, although Nussbaum has since repudiated her version of the argument.

avoid these things, prevent them, minimize them, cope with them, overcome them, learn from them, and survive them, and the extent to which these efforts constrain our choices and define our priorities. All the concepts I have mentioned—loss, illness, injury, harm, risk, and danger—derive much of their content from our standing recognition that our lives are temporally bounded, that we are subject to death at any moment, and that we are certain to succumb to it in the end. In a life without death, the meaning of all these concepts would be called into question. Yet without them, it is equally unclear what would be meant by such concepts as those of health, gain, safety, security, and benefit. And it is not easy to form a picture of human deliberation in which none of these concepts played any role. If we assume—and I do not think it is a trivial assumption— that immortal beings would continue to be susceptible to pleasure and pain, then perhaps there would be scope for them to deploy rudimentary hedonistic concepts of gain and loss in their deliberations, but the character of those deliberations would still be radically different from our own.[13]

To this point I have been taking immortality to involve, as Williams himself initially does, "living as an embodied person in the world rather as it is" (90), only doing so forever. One of the conclusions suggested by the considerations I have been rehearsing is that we can make little sense of immortality understood in this way. On

---

13. I am taking it for granted, both here and in what follows, that the situation we are now contemplating is one in which all human beings are immortal. But suppose that there were only one immortal person and that everyone else continued to age and die in the usual way. Then the risks and dangers to other people whom the immortal loved might render him vicariously vulnerable to harm and injury and so make greater deliberative complexity possible. Of course, the kinds of attachments that an immortal creature might form to mere mortals are open to speculation. Speculation of this sort is responsible for much of the imaginative power of ancient Greek mythology and, if my arguments are correct, it is doubtful whether there could be a comparably rich mythology that was limited exclusively to interactions among immortals.

the most basic level, we have no clear way of understanding the biology of it. This is already implicit in the story of EM, and it emerges forcefully if we consider the question of how she is to be represented as a character in a staged performance. Relative to the normal human life span, a 342-year-old woman is of course extraordinarily old, which might suggest that she should be represented as someone exceedingly feeble and ancient. But relative to her potentially eternal existence, she is of course extraordinarily young, and so perhaps she should instead be represented as the freshest possible newborn infant. Neither of these possibilities seems especially promising from a dramatic point of view, and hence as a matter of stagecraft the decision to present her as eternally 42 is extremely judicious. But of course even this requires that the immortality in question should be understood as unidirectional. It is a life that has no end but nevertheless has a beginning. Otherwise we could not make sense of the idea of EM's being either 42 or 342 or any other age, nor could we give any answer, in biological terms, to the awkward question of where she had come from.

Problems such as these put pressure on us to move, as many have in any case wanted to move, toward a reconceptualization of immortality as involving a kind of noncorporeal existence which would be sufficiently unlike ordinary life on earth as to sidestep these issues. But to suspend in this way all the constraints imposed by our biology—by our nature as organisms—is to make it even clearer that we are no longer thinking of a human life in any recognizable sense at all. We are somehow imagining creatures who are meant to be like us but who are not embodied in the way we are, who pass through no stages of life, who know nothing of the characteristic challenges, triumphs, or disasters associated with any of those stages, who need not work to survive, who do not undergo danger or overcome it, who do not age or face death or the risk of it, who do not experience the reactions of grief and loss that the death of a loved one inspires, and who never have to make what they can of the limited time and opportunities that they have been given. More generally, we are trying to imagine creatures who have little in their existence that matches our experience of tragic or even difficult choices, and nothing at all that matches our experience of decisions made against the background of the limits imposed by the ultimate scarce resource, time. But *every* human decision is made against that background, and so in imagining immortality we are imagining an existence in which there are, effectively, no human decisions.

Nor, accordingly, is it clear what place there is for human values in such an existence, for consider the extent to which our assignments of value are a response to the limits of time. Those limits, and especially the constraints they impose upon us in contexts of decision, force upon us the need to establish priorities, to guide our lives under a conception of which things are worth doing and caring about and choosing. Without such limits, it is at best unclear how far we would be guided by ideas of value at all. John Rawls used the phrase "the circumstances of justice" to refer to the conditions, such as moderate scarcity of resources, under which justice emerges as a virtue and there is a need for its norms.[14] We might, by analogy, use the phrase "the circumstances of value" to refer to the conditions under which the attitude of valuing comes to play an important role in human life. And prominent among those conditions, I am suggesting, is temporal scarcity.[15]

14. See John Rawls, *A Theory of Justice* (Cambridge: Harvard University Press, 1971), 126–30.

15. Immortality would not eliminate all forms of temporal scarcity from human life. Even if we were all immortal, for example, we would still have only a limited amount of time in which to engage with any objects (paintings, mountains, etc.) that were themselves of finite duration or to witness or participate in any events that were nonrepeating. These forms of scarcity might create some pressure to develop and deploy concepts of value, but I believe that this pressure would be much weaker than the pressure exerted by our own mortality. And in creating even this weaker sort of pressure, they would, of course, confirm the general link between temporal scarcity and valuation.

When we are tempted, as many of us are at times, to wish that our lives could go on forever, often what we are wishing is that some version of the lives we are now leading could continue without end: an improved version, perhaps, but a recognizable version nonetheless. If what I have been saying is even roughly correct, however, the wish is confused. It is essential to our idea of a life that it is temporally bounded, with a beginning, a middle, and an end, and with stages of development defining its normal trajectory. A life without temporal boundaries would no more be a life than a circle without a circumference would be a circle. So whatever the eternal existence of a being might be like, it would not be just like our lives only more so. The statement that death is essential to our concept of a life is not merely a trivial truth resting on a stipulative definition of "life." It is a substantive observation which reminds us that the aspects of life that we cherish most dearly—love and labor, intimacy and achievement, creativity and humor and solidarity and all the rest—all have the status of *values* for us because of their role in our finite and bounded lives. The point is not merely that without death we would not have what we are accustomed to thinking of as lives, although that is certainly true; the more important point is that our confidence in the values that make our lives worth living depends on the place of the things that we value in the lives of temporally bounded creatures like ourselves. Rather than giving us an eternity to relish those things, immortality would undermine the conditions of our valuing them in the first place.[16]

16. The idea that *confidence*, rather than knowledge or decision, may provide the most defensible basis for evaluative conviction in modern conditions is an important theme of Bernard Williams's *Ethics and the Limits of Philosophy* (London: Fontana Press/Collins, 1985). Williams had in mind ethical values in particular, and his emphasis was on confidence as a social phenomenon: a social state that may be fostered by some kinds of "institutions, upbringing, and public discourse" (*Ethics and the Limits of Philosophy*, 20) and not by others. The arguments I have been developing in this book serve as a reminder that values of all kinds, and not only ethical values, must attract our confidence if

I have been arguing that our confidence in our values depends on our status as mortals who lead temporally bounded lives and that immortality would undermine that confidence. This argument provides a different route to Williams's conclusion that death gives the meaning to life. However, this conclusion can sound odd or even absurd. It may seem to suggest that we should *welcome* death or at any rate not fear it. As such, it may strike some people as being just another vain attempt to use metaphysics to fight fear. But the inference from the role of death in securing the meaning of our lives to the unreasonableness of fearing it is not obvious. After all, it is not unheard of that we should have reason to fear things even though we recognize that our lives would be worse without them. Think, for example, of going to the dentist, leaving home for the first time, or undertaking risky but rewarding activities more generally. Certainly there is nothing about the role of death in supporting our confidence in our values that precludes our wishing that it came considerably later than it does. And, as earlier noted, Williams himself explicitly leaves open the possibility that we may have reason to fear death even if we recognize its role in securing the meaningfulness of our lives. Still, this is an awkward combination of attitudes. Death is perceived by many people as uniquely terrifying. To accept that the perception is reasonable while simultaneously recognizing that immortality would be undesirable is, at the very least, a strange and unsettling position in which to find oneself.

In fact, I think that we are justified in holding a combination of attitudes that is in some ways even more unsettling than this. But before explaining why, let me dwell a little longer on the reasonableness of fear. *Should* we agree that it is reasonable to fear death? The Second Epicurean Conclusion delivers a negative answer to this question. The Epicurean hypothesis is that the fear of death is

they are to play a role in our lives, and that it is not only social institutions and practices, but also wider features of human life and experience, that can either support such confidence or undermine it.

really the fear of the imagined experience of being dead. Epicurus's argument exposes this as a confusion: there is no experience of being dead, and so there is nothing to fear. Unlike some people, I don't think that this diagnosis is completely implausible. I believe that more people than might care to admit it are subject to something that might be described as a fear of the experience of being dead. This fear reveals itself, perhaps, when people wish to be buried near their loved ones so that they won't be lonely in death, or when they prefer cheerful and picturesque settings for their burial plots rather than gloomy or depressing ones. What is implausible is just the idea that the Epicurean diagnosis is complete: that the only thing that people fear, in fearing death, is the supposed experience of being dead. It seems clear that, for many people at least, there is more than this involved. As indicated earlier, however, I do not think that the deprivation theory provides a natural way of accounting for the remainder, even though it is true that people do sometimes fear that death will deprive them of the opportunity to witness or participate in some eagerly anticipated event. Again, the point is not that people are never subject to fears of this kind, but merely that such fears are not exhaustive. There is something else that many people find distinctively terrifying about the prospect of their own deaths.

But are they reasonable to do so? For my part, I have a hard time seeing why not, assuming that they are glad to be alive and would like to go on living. I have already suggested that the type of fear that many people experience when contemplating their own deaths is a special sort of panic induced by the prospect that the egocentric subject—the subject of all one's thoughts and attitudes, including the very attitudes one is experiencing as one contemplates one's death—will cease to exist. The panic is compounded by the recognition that all of one's other attitudes—including one's attitudes toward other instances of loss and deprivation—have taken for granted the persistence of the self whose nonpersistence is precisely what is now being contemplated and is itself the object of the very attitudes that one is now having. If fear is paradigmatically a response to a perceived threat or danger, and if it is not unreasonable to perceive the unwanted cessation of one's existence as a threat, then the fear of death is not (or at any rate need not be) unreasonable.

Some people, using metaphysics to fight fear, will argue that the idea of a persistent egocentric subject that figures in this account is an illusion, so that the fear of death is unwarranted to the extent that it presupposes such a subject. I find this view incredible, but I will not discuss it here, except to say that in order for it to succeed in demonstrating the unreasonableness of fearing death, it must show not merely that there is no egocentric subject in the relevant sense but that people are unreasonable to think that there is. Otherwise, the fear of death might be reasonable even if it presupposed a metaphysics of the self that was in fact false. There is also the point that, if the argument does succeed, it succeeds by demonstrating that we cannot cease to exist because, in the relevant sense, we never existed in the first place, and it is then an open question how it is reasonable to respond to *that* piece of information. Some will wonder whether it is any more comforting to contemplate the fact of our current nonexistence than it is to contemplate the prospect of our ceasing to exist in the future.

Rather than appealing to considerations about the nature of the self to dispute the reasonableness of fearing death, there is an argument that appeals to considerations about the nature of fear. The argument I have in mind begins with the claim that, insofar as fear is capable of being either reasonable or unreasonable, it is always a propositional attitude, an attitude which takes a proposition as its object. Propositional fear, the argument asserts, is to be distinguished from the *state* of fear, which is an involuntary state of physiological arousal that is neither reasonable nor unreasonable.[17]

17. In sketching the view of fear discussed in this paragraph, I have followed with some modifications the position developed by Robert Gordon in

The language in which we describe our fears sometimes makes their propositional character explicit by the use of "that" clauses which identify the relevant propositional objects. For example, we may say we are afraid *that we will be unable to pay the rent* or *that we will lose our job*. But often the object of our fear is propositional even when our language does not make this explicit. We may say, for example, that we are afraid *of failing the test* or *of an explosion*, but in these cases the real object of our fear is *that we will fail the test* or *that there will be an explosion*. Propositional fear, the argument continues, is an attitude that we can experience only when we are uncertain whether the thing we fear will come to pass. In this sense, such fear is always a response to uncertainty. For example, if I am certain that I will have to undergo a painful medical procedure, then I cannot be afraid that I will have to undergo a painful medical procedure, although of course I may well be very unhappy about it. Similarly, if I am certain that I will be unable to pay the rent, then I cannot fear that I will be unable to pay the rent, although my inability to pay may well make me miserable. Now it may be said to follow from this uncertainty requirement that it is never reasonable to fear death. I cannot reasonably fear that I will die someday because I am certain that I will die someday.[18] To be sure, the prospect of dying may on occasion cause me to experience involuntary physiological responses such as sweating, rapid heartbeat, and so on, but these involuntary responses, which are constitutive of the nonpropositional state of fear, are neither reasonable nor unreasonable.

"Fear," *The Philosophical Review* 89 (1980): 560–78. (See also Wayne Davis, "The Varieties of Fear," *Philosophical Studies* 51 [1987]: 287–310.) In thinking about the bearing of this view of fear on questions about death, I have benefited from an unpublished paper by Katrina Przyjemski. See also O. H. Green, "Fear of Death," *Philosophy and Phenomenological Research* 43 (1982): 99–105.

18. Shelly Kagan endorses this view in his book *Death* (New Haven, CT: Yale University Press, 2012), 297.

I find it implausible that fear must always take one of the two forms suggested: that it must either be a propositional attitude that is subject to the uncertainty requirement or else be an involuntary physiological state that is insensitive to reasons. Imagine that I am in the dentist's chair awaiting a scheduled procedure. The dentist comes in and tells me that the procedure will begin in a few minutes and that 50 percent of those who undergo this procedure find it extremely painful. He then leaves the room. The view under consideration allows that, in his absence, I may be subject to two kinds of fear. I may experience propositional fear that that the procedure will be extremely painful, and I may find myself in a state of involuntary physiological arousal characterized by sweaty palms, rapid heartbeat, and all the rest. Now suppose that the dentist returns and tells me that he was mistaken about which procedure I am to undergo. The actual procedure is one that 100 percent of patients find extremely painful. As a result of his saying this, I am now certain that I will find the procedure extremely painful. On the proposed view, my propositional fear must disappear; I can no longer fear that the procedure will be painful, for I am certain that it will be. And while my state of fear may persist or even intensify, it cannot be described as either reasonable or unreasonable, for it is merely an involuntary state of physiological arousal. But this is implausible. It may be true that I can no longer be afraid *that the procedure is going to be painful.* But I might nevertheless say that I am afraid *of the procedure,* and if asked why I am afraid of the procedure, I might say that I am afraid of it because I am certain that it is going to be painful. In saying these things, I would not merely be reporting a state of physiological arousal. I would instead be expressing an attitude that was sensitive to reasons. I regard the dentist's utterance as providing me with a reason for my fearful attitude, and if I came to believe that it was not a reason—say because the giggling in the corridor led me to realize that the dentist's prediction of pain had just been a sadistic April Fool's joke—then my attitude would disappear. Either this reason-sensitive attitude can somehow be interpreted as a form of propositional fear,[19] in which case such fear is not always subject to the uncertainty requirement, or else it is a form of nonpropositional fear, in which case such fears can indeed be reasonable. And so it is, I believe, with the fear of death. Perhaps we cannot have the propositional fear *that we are going to die* since we are certain that we are going to die. But we may nevertheless be afraid *of dying* or *of death*, and these fears are not merely involuntary physiological states that are insensitive to reasons.

Suppose, however, that I am wrong about this. Suppose that the proposed view of fear is correct, and that we cannot have a fear of death that is either reasonable or unreasonable. Even if this is so, there are many other reason-sensitive attitudes we may have toward death that are not subject to the uncertainty condition and are equally inconsistent with the spirit of the Second Epicurean Conclusion. For example, we may dread our deaths, despite being certain that they will occur, just as we may dread a painful medical procedure that we are certain we will have to undergo. Dread is not subject to the uncertainty condition. We may also be horrified or aghast at the prospect of our deaths. It would be a hollow vindication of Epicureanism, which aspires to free us from mental distress and enable us to attain *ataraxia,* to demonstrate that we cannot fear our own deaths but can only dread them or be horrified or aghast at them. This would hardly show that death "is nothing to us." My own view, then, is that it is reasonable to fear death, and I will proceed on that assumption, but if some are inclined to argue, along the lines I have been considering, that we can only dread death and cannot fear it, then they can make the appropriate substitutions in what follows.

So we are, I believe, in the strange and unsettling position that I described earlier. It is not unreasonable to fear death, even if one

---

19. The idea of a "reason-sensitive attitude" is similar to Scanlon's notion of a "judgment-sensitive attitude," of which he takes fear to be an example. See *What We Owe to Each Other,* 20.

recognizes that immortality would be undesirable and that there is a sense in which death gives the meaning to life. In fact, as I said earlier, my own view is that we are justified in holding a combination of attitudes that is in some ways even more unsettling than this. Let me explain why. I argued in "The Afterlife" that, even though the prospect of our own mortality poses little threat to our confidence in what we value, the prospect of human beings as a whole dying out poses a very great threat. Without confidence that others will live on after we ourselves have died, many of the things that now matter to us would cease to do so or would come to matter less. We saw, for example, that many projects, such as trying to find a cure for cancer, are undertaken with the understanding that their ultimate goals may not be achieved during one's own lifetime. That such projects can nevertheless seem compelling to us reveals that what happens after we are dead matters a great deal to us. It matters enough that we think it can be worthwhile to devote one's life to an undertaking even though its primary payoff is expected to be achieved only after one is gone. To put the point in terms of Williams's earlier distinction, our desires that these projects should succeed are neither conditional on our being alive nor are they categorical in a sense which implies that their fulfillment depends on our remaining alive. The desires can be satisfied even if we die, and the prospect of our death does not deprive the projects of their perceived value or prevent them from being important to us now. By contrast, if we were faced with the imminent disappearance of the human race, then these projects would seem pointless. They would cease to matter to us or to seem worth pursuing.

Nor, as we saw, is it only goal-oriented projects like trying to cure cancer whose capacity to attract our interest and engagement depends on the assumption that human life will continue after we ourselves are dead. The perceived value of many other activities seems similarly to depend on our confidence that humanity will survive, and the prospect of humanity's imminent disappearance would pose a wide-ranging threat to our ability, here and now, to lead value-laden lives—lives structured by wholehearted engagement in valued activities and pursuits. Rather than repeating my arguments for these claims, however, I want to explain how my conclusions about the collective afterlife bear on the primary question I have been concerned with in this lecture, namely, the question of what attitudes it is reasonable to have toward one's death.

I said earlier that to fear one's own death even while recognizing that immortality would be undesirable is a strange and unsettling combination of attitudes, albeit a combination we may nevertheless be justified in having. But if I am right that, like personal immortality, the imminent disappearance of human life on earth would also tend to erode our evaluative confidence, then, as I indicated, the combination of attitudes that we are justified in holding may in fact be even more unsettling. On the one hand, the fear of death is for many people uniquely intense, and, if I am right, it need not be unreasonable. On the other hand, our ability to lead value-laden lives is not only compatible with the fact that we will die but actually depends on it. What it is not compatible with is the prospect that human life on earth will disappear soon *after* we are dead. So although our fear of death may be reasonable, our confidence in our values depends far more on our confidence in the survival of other people after our deaths than it does on our confidence in our own survival. Indeed, our own eternal survival would itself undermine such confidence. To put it a bit too simply: what is necessary to sustain our confidence in our values is that we should die and that others should live. But this does not mean that we should regard our own deaths with equanimity, although some of us may, or that we should cease to fear death if we are among those who do fear it. The fear of death is not undermined by the considerations about confidence that I have mentioned.

It may be wondered why, if temporal scarcity with respect to individual survival is among the circumstances of value, the same is not true of temporal scarcity with respect to humanity's survival? If our confidence in our values depends on our recognition that we as individuals lead finite and bounded lives, why should that very same confidence be threatened by a recognition of humanity's temporal limits? The answer, I take it, is that our recognition of our own individual mortality exerts a formative influence on our attitudes as individual subjects and, in particular, forces upon us the need to guide our lives under a conception of which things are worth doing and caring about and choosing. In so doing, it is implicated in the formation and development of our ideas of value from the outset. The recognition of humanity's temporal limits plays no such role. On the one hand, it is not implicated in the evaluative thought of individuals in the same way. To the contrary, I have argued that our confidence in humanity's survival— if not forever then at least for an indefinitely long period of time—is an unstated precondition for our confidence as individuals in the value of many our activities. On the other hand, humanity as a whole is not a unified subject with attitudes of its own: attitudes that might, by analogy to the individual case, be shaped by a recognition of humanity's finite and bounded existence. So while temporal scarcity at the individual level exerts a formative and pervasive influence on individual human experience and on the attitudes associated with human valuing, there is no unified agent at any level with attitudes that are similarly shaped by the recognition of temporal scarcity as it applies to humanity as a whole.

My conclusion, then, is that we find ourselves in the following strange and unsettling position. In part, our confidence depends on the very thing we fear. We fear death, but it is needed to sustain our confidence in the importance of what we value. And we may recognize its role in sustaining our confidence, but that does not mean we are unreasonable to fear it. At the same time, our confidence also depends on the continuity of human life. It depends, in particular, on the persistence of human life after our own deaths, which matters more to us than we sometimes recognize. If one wanted to put the point in terms of Janáček's operas, one might say that the lessons of *The Makropulos Case* go hand-in-hand with those of *The Cunning Little Vixen*.[20]

If what I have been arguing is correct, it follows that our confidence in our values depends both on death, which is inevitable and which many of us nevertheless fear, and on the survival of human life, which is not at all inevitable and threats to which most of us do not fear enough. We do not fear them enough both in the sense that greater fear is warranted, because the threats are grave, and in the sense that greater fear would serve a useful function, because the threats might be overcome if we were motivated to try. Yet we fear what we cannot prevent, even though it does not threaten our confidence, and we fail to fear what we might be able to prevent, even though it does threaten our confidence. It is at this point, I believe, and only at this point, that our complex attitudes toward death begin to shade over from the merely strange and unsettling to the unreasonable. We are not unreasonable for fearing death, even though it does not threaten our confidence. But we may be unreasonable if we fail sufficiently to fear, and so do not try to overcome, the ever more serious threats to humanity's survival, upon which our confidence does depend. This is a significant conclusion in its own right, and it also tells us something interesting about the relation between fear and confidence. It is natural to suppose that these two attitudes always work against one another. But when, as in the case of humanity's survival, the sources of our confidence are themselves under threat, then by motivating us to address those threats, the tendency of fear may be to support confidence rather than to undermine it. With the fear of death, things are different. In that case, as I have said, we fear the very thing on which our confidence depends, and it would be going too far to say that the one attitude supports the other. What is nevertheless true, however, is that the intensity of our fear testifies to the depth of our confidence in the value of all that death brings to an end.

20. See Lecture 2, n. 3.

Comments

The Significance of Doomsday

Susan Wolf

Virtually all of us take it for granted that human life will go on long after we are gone. How long? Hundreds of years? Thousands of years? Tens of thousands? Hundreds of thousands? The fact that many of us are vague about how many zeroes to tack on to the answer shows how little we are accustomed to considering the matter. Nonetheless, I suspect that virtually all of us are confident that, at any rate, humanity will go on for *a good long time*. In his fascinating and deeply original Tanner Lectures, "The Afterlife," Samuel Scheffler speculates on the role this assumption plays in the formation and sustenance of our values and in the activities that structure our lives, and he explores the significance it would have for our self-understanding if his speculations are right.

With Scheffler, I believe that our confidence in the continuation of the human race plays an *enormous*, if mostly tacit, role in the way we conceive of our activities and understand their value. With Scheffler, I agree that if we were to lose this confidence, our lives would change radically, and much for the worse. Still, my conjectures about how they would change, my interest in the question of how it would be reasonable for them to change, and the conclusions I am inclined to draw from the answers to these questions about the relation of our values to our belief in posterity are somewhat different.

Scheffler begins by asking us to consider a doomsday scenario in which each of us is to imagine learning that although we ourselves will live to the end of our natural lifespans, thirty days after our death the earth will collide with a giant asteroid and be destroyed.

Later he offers a variation of this thought experiment, based on a novel by P. D. James and a subsequent film directed by Alfonso Cuarón, in which humans have become infertile.[1] After taking us through a series of imagined reactions to different types of activities and values, Scheffler suggests, in keeping with James and Cuarón, that a world in which the demise of humanity is known to be imminent would be "characterized by widespread apathy, anomie, and despair; by the erosion of social institutions and social solidarity; by the deterioration of the physical environment; and by a pervasive loss of conviction about the value or point of many activities" (40). Calling this, or something like it, "the afterlife conjecture," Scheffler draws out what he takes this conjecture to imply.

Scheffler is rightly cautious in his conclusions, acknowledging that his predictions are but conjectures. Still, it might be worthwhile to explicitly acknowledge how ill-equipped we are to make reliable judgments about this. The question of how we would react to the prospect of imminent extinction appears to be an empirical question, which philosophers and novelists are not especially well placed to answer. But with respect to this issue, I would not place much credence in the conclusions of psychologists or social scientists either. Although they could conduct surveys and experiments, asking large numbers of people how they *think* they would react or even, perhaps, simulating environments in which the subjects half-believe that the doomsday or infertility scenario is true, they could at best get evidence for predicting people's first and early reactions to this. We are not very good at predicting our reactions to changes in deeply ingrained habits or beliefs, and it seems reasonable to expect that a change in a belief as deeply ingrained and

---

1. In this variant, the doom is more gradual, as people slowly die out. Furthermore, in this variant the planet survives, even though humanity does not. There are interesting questions to be explored about the differences between these scenarios, and how these differences might affect our responses to them, but these are not Scheffler's focus nor will they be mine.

fundamental as the belief in posterity would take considerable time to integrate into a stably revised worldview.[2]

This will not keep me from adding my own conjectures to those of Scheffler and James and Cuarón. I am as comfortable in my armchair as the next philosopher (or philosophical novelist). But my own conjectures about how we *would* react are inextricable from thoughts about how we *should* react—that is, thoughts about how it would be *reasonable* to react. Although Scheffler shies away from this more prescriptive question, I find it irresistible. My conjectures are thus to some extent unavoidably informed by my unreflective intuitions about what would be reasonable. After offering some of these conjectures, I shall also raise some prescriptive questions explicitly.

1. The Nature and Limits of Egoism

Let me begin, however, with a question that grants Scheffler the likelihood of his afterlife conjecture and asks about his interpretation of what the truth of that conjecture would imply. Noting that we would regard the extinction of humanity with more horror than we do our own deaths, and that we would find it harder, if not impossible, to live meaningful lives under this assumption than we do under the acknowledgment of our personal mortality, Scheffler concludes, "In certain concrete functional and motivational respects, the fact that we and everyone we love will cease to exist matters

2. When the practice of women's choosing to keep their own surnames after marriage was new, people predicted (quite wrongly, in my experience) that it would be very complicated and confusing for others. Indeed, many still make these mistaken predictions. People also predicted that having to separate out paper and plastic for recycling would be very troublesome, but now it is second nature for many. A more apt comparison to the present case might be the speculations people living in a nearly universal Christian society made about the consequences of losing faith.

less to us than would the nonexistence of future people whom we do not know and who, indeed, have no determinate identities. Or to put it more positively, the coming into existence of people we do not know and love matters more to us than our own survival and the survival of the people we do know and love." He takes this to reflect something both striking and surprising about "the nature and limits of our personal egoism" (45).

Although I agree with Scheffler that, in certain respects, the survival of humanity is more important to us than our own survival, and agree, on entirely independent grounds, that people are much less egoistic than some philosophers and economists make us out to be, it is unclear to me how the first point, or the afterlife conjecture from which it derives, provides any particular support for the second.

Though I don't think that most people are (either purely or dominantly) egoistic, I do think that some people are. Donald Trump, perhaps, or Mike Tyson or a contemporary nonfictional Don Juan. In the spirit of the afterlife conjecture, I can easily imagine that upon learning that the end of the world is near, any one of these individuals might lose interest in the activities and pursuits that until then made his life exciting and fun. What's the point, one of them might wonder, of being the richest man in the world, or the heavyweight champ, or the world's most impressive seducer, if the world will come to an end in thirty or fifty years? But would this reaction show these characters to be any less egoistic than they seemed to us before? I don't see how. What it does show rather is, first, that self-concern on any but the most hedonistic conception is not to be identified with a concern for maximizing one's survival or even one's pleasure,[3] and second, that many of the goals and states the realization of which *would* answer to one's self-concern are parasitic on the existence of other people, including, as the afterlife

3. This is connected to Scheffler's point that our values are nonexperientialist (20).

conjecture particularly reflects, of other people who live on after we are gone.[4]

This is clearest in cases in which fame, prestige, and other competitive goals figure into a person's conception of the good—and in which, whether consciously or subconsciously, one's ambitions for such things extend beyond the present generation. But if, as the afterlife conjecture plausibly suggests, even "the appetitive pleasures of food, drink, and sex might be affected" (42), I don't see why this should be taken to imply that the individual's *interest* in food, drink, and sex is any less egoistic than it would have been if the gourmand, the glutton, or the stud were unmoved by the prospect of doomsday and carried on as gleefully as before. According to the afterlife conjecture as I understand it, the prospect of doomsday would, to quote Huckleberry Finn, "take the tuck all out of [us]."[5] It would unsettle us, making many of our goals and values seem shallow, and so less satisfying to achieve. But this wouldn't show that our goals and values are any more, or any less, egoistic, than they seemed before—it would only show that happiness would, on the doomsday scenario, be harder for an egoist to achieve.

Since Scheffler is careful to qualify his claims about the comparative strengths of our interest in ourselves and in others with phrases like "a very specific sense" and "in certain concrete . . . respects" (73, 45), he and I may not really disagree. Moreover, he takes the afterlife conjecture to show us something about "the nature *and* limits of our egoism" (45, emphasis added)—if we place the stress on "nature" rather than on "limits," my remarks may even be understood to complement his own. For, as I have mentioned, the afterlife conjecture does make clear that even egoists are not solipsists, or, in Scheffler's vocabulary, individualists (about value), and that many

4. This is connected to Scheffler's point that our values are not individualist (59–60).

5. Mark Twain, *The Adventures of Huckleberry Finn* (New York: Charles L. Webster and Co., 1885), ch. XVI.

of our egoistic concerns are dependent on the existence and attention of others, including, probably more than we realize, the existence of others who exist long after we have died.

2. *An Alternative Afterlife Conjecture*

Few people, however, are as egoistic as I am imagining Donald Trump and Mike Tyson to be, so let us set them aside and accept Scheffler's invitation to speculate on how the rest of us would react to the doomsday or the infertility scenario. When I engage in these speculations, I find myself wondering whether Scheffler's afterlife conjecture—or, more specifically, that part of it that predicts "widespread apathy" and "anomie" (40)—is ultimately significantly more plausible than an alternative one, in which our reaction to extinction is less dispiriting.

As Scheffler points out, the prospect of imminent extinction would immediately give us reason to abandon many of our current activities and projects—in some cases, by rendering their goals unattainable, and in others, by undermining the value or point of attaining them. The fact that the prospect of extinction would call for changes of this sort, however, is not in any obvious way philosophically surprising. We always have reason to change our projects when circumstances arise that render them pointless: If the place one had planned to go to for a holiday is flattened by a hurricane, one must find a new destination. If the company one works for goes out of business, one must find a new job. And if the people you were counting on to help you with your projects or whom your projects were aimed at pleasing or helping will be destroyed or aborted by the planet's collision with a giant asteroid—well, you had better find something else to do with your time.[6] But what?

---

6. Scheffler appears to address this reaction when he writes, against those who would say "this mundane point about instrumental rationality is all that is

After considering the wide variety of projects that would manifestly be rendered pointless by imminent extinction, Scheffler discusses a range of activities and goals with respect to which the relevance of extinction is less obvious or direct. Regarding creative and scholarly projects, for example, he asks "Would artistic, musical, and literary projects still seem worth undertaking? Would humanistic scholars continue to be motivated to engage in basic research? Would historians and theoretical physicists and anthropologists all carry on as before? Perhaps, but the answer is not obvious" (25). By the time Scheffler offers the afterlife conjecture, his speculations have grown more pessimistic.

Insofar as the afterlife conjecture is a plausible one—and, with Scheffler, James, and Cuarón, I believe that it is—we have here reached something of great philosophical interest. *Why* would our interest in theoretical research and in artistic expression weaken? One answer that would make this reaction intelligible is that when artists create, scholars write, and scientists do research, they are hoping to produce work that will be enjoyed and esteemed for many generations. But this seems unlikely, and even the less grandiose hope of producing work that will at any rate have a small and possibly unrecognized effect on the direction and character of their fields seems more than most artists and scholars would insist on. If, as I think, for most artists and scholars, at least in the humanities, it would be profoundly gratifying for one's work to be found useful or beautiful or worthwhile by even a small portion of one's own generation, then it is puzzling why the absence of subsequent

needed to explain why people would no longer regard such projects as worth pursuing," that "this misconstrues the significance of the example" (27). "What may be surprising," he goes on to say, "is the fact that people are often happy to pursue goals that they do not expect to be achieved until after their own deaths" (27). As it happens, this does not seem particularly surprising to me, but, as I go on to say, the likelihood that some of our other activities and goals may be undermined by the prospect of our imminent extinction does strike me as surprising and deeply philosophically puzzling.

generations should take the sails out of one's efforts. Even more puzzling, if the afterlife conjecture is right, is why the doomsday scenario would weaken the motivations of practitioners of the performing arts. Would the prospect of human extinction weaken our motivation to play piano, to act, to dance?

Puzzling as it is, I don't deny that the prospect of doomsday might affect us this way. As a *first* reaction to the scenario, indeed, it seems to me quite natural that it would. Having the confidence we do that our species and even our society will continue long after we are gone, we tend implicitly to conceive of our activities as entering or as being parts of one or another ongoing stream—of the history and community of art or of science; of an ethnic or religious culture; of legal, political, industrial, technological developments, and so on. This feature of the way we conceive of activities, unconscious and unarticulated though it may be, may well play a significant role in the meaning and value these activities have for us. Even if we do not think of ourselves as affecting the direction or shape of these streams, the mere fact that we are contributing to them gives us a place in or attachment to a larger and independently valuable whole.[7] Learning that the streams we thought our activities were a part of would be coming abruptly to an end would profoundly shift our understanding of what we have been doing; it would shake the foundations on which the meaningfulness and value of these activities rested.

The idea that the expectation of our imminent extinction would profoundly *shift* our understanding of our activities and *shake* the foundations of their having meaning and value for us seems plausible to me. But would it utterly destroy their meaning and value? It is not obvious to me that it would.

---

7. I argue that engagement in activities that connect us in a positive way to things of independent value are crucial to living meaningful lives in *Meaning in Lives and Why It Matters* (Princeton, NJ: Princeton University Press, 2010).

At least twice in the course of his speculations about how many of our ordinary concerns would weaken or disappear under the shadow of imminent extinction, Scheffler acknowledges the likelihood that a few values and interests would remain. In Lecture 1, he mentions that "the projects and activities that would seem least likely to be affected by the doomsday scenario are those focused on personal comfort and pleasure," (though he rightly adds that "it is...not altogether obvious what would be comforting and pleasant under doomsday conditions") (25). In Lecture 2, he admits that "Even in an infertile world, it seems plausible to suppose that it would be important to people to be free from severe pain...Nor, similarly, does it seem likely that friendship and other close personal relations would cease to matter to people" (54). In fact, what seems *to me* the least likely sort of activity to be affected by the doomsday scenario might be thought of as an integration or synthesis of these remarks: The sorts of activities least likely to be affected by the doomsday or infertility scenario are those that are explicitly focused on the care and comfort of others.

It is a striking fact how much time and money and effort we are willing to spend on the care of those who are close to us—not just care for our children, but, when we reach a certain age, care for our parents as well (and, of course, for our spouses, our siblings, and our friends, when they are in need of our care). Our devotion includes and perhaps especially extends to our loved ones who are dying. In cases where it is vivid to us that our loved ones will die soon and that they have little chance of contributing more to the communities and institutions of which they have been a part, it seems least likely that the doomsday scenario will make any difference to us. Even if doomsday threatens to send us into a depression and sap our enthusiasm for everything else, the concern to comfort those in immediate need of care is likely to make us resist giving in. This suggests the possibility of an alternative conjecture to the dystopian one that James, Cuarón, and eventually Scheffler propose. Specifically, it suggests the possibility that once the immediate shock of our imminent extinction has worn off and we have come to accept it, we also come to recognize that we are, so to speak, "all in this together," a single community on this sinking ship of a planet. And as we come to think of our fellow humans in this way, perhaps we will find ourselves moved to provide the same care for each other that we have shown ourselves so ready to lavish on our dying or despairing relatives and friends.

For empirical evidence about the likelihood of this, it would be helpful to know how people behave on literally sinking ships, downed submarines, or space shuttle missions that have gone disastrously wrong so as to isolate their crews, with nothing to look forward to but their collective annihilation. It seems to me at least possible that with the right leadership, such groups would remain motivated to think and act and care for each other right to the end, and that, analogously, with the right leadership, we, too, if faced with imminent extinction, could resist the tendency toward apathy and anomie portrayed in the afterlife conjecture, and think and act and care for each other. Moreover, since we would have time and resources that these other groups lack,[8] we would have a wide range of means for caring and comforting each other at our disposal. We could create and perform music and plays, we could plant gardens, hold discussion groups, write books and commentaries. Being motivated at first to help and comfort each other, we might find ourselves reengaged by the beauty, the challenge, and the interest these projects held for us in our predoomsday lives. In other words, in helping each other, we might help ourselves.

I do not say that we would be happy. Even on this conjecture, much less pessimistic than Scheffler's, I share Scheffler's doubt "that there is something [available in this community on the brink of extinction] that we would be prepared to count as a good life" (43). But even if, under the circumstances, we would not be in a

---

8. We would have even more resources than we have now, in fact, since on that scenario we would have no reason to make efforts at conservation.

position to live a good life or a happy one, we could, on this conjecture, at least live a meaningful one.

Up to a point, my speculations and alternative afterlife conjecture follow and agree with Scheffler's. My remarks about seeing ourselves as contributors to ongoing "streams," for example, echo his reflections in Lecture 2:

> Our concerns and commitments, our values and judgments of importance, our sense of what matters and what is worth doing—all these things are formed and sustained against a background in which it is taken for granted that human life is itself a thriving, ongoing enterprise. Many of our deepest and most defining values and aspirations and ambitions...depend on our taking this for granted. In fact, we take it so much for granted that we seldom recognize its role...But this does nothing to diminish its significance. Humanity itself as an ongoing, historical project provides the implicit frame of reference for most of our judgments about what matters. Remove that frame of reference, and our sense of importance...is destabilized and begins to erode. (59–60)

Where I suggest, however, that our destabilization might be temporary, and that we might, as a result of a robust concern to mitigate the despair and apathy of others, pull ourselves back from the brink of our own despair, Scheffler voices no such hope. To the contrary, he writes, "We need humanity to have a future if many of our own individual purposes are to matter to us now. Indeed, I believe that something stronger is true: we need humanity to have a future for the very idea that things *matter* to retain a secure place in our conceptual repertoire" (60).[9]

If my alternative afterlife conjecture is plausible—it need not be *more* plausible than Scheffler's, just plausible—and my description of the people imagined in it as living meaningful, even if not happy, lives is coherent, then it seems that Scheffler's final claim about the

9. Of course, if humanity does not have a future, neither does our conceptual repertoire. But we may leave this point to one side.

reliance of the very idea of things mattering on posterity cannot be right. An alternative hypothesis, compatible with Scheffler's anti-individualism about values, but also with my somewhat less pessimistic afterlife scenario, is that the very idea that things matter relies on a valuing community (of more than one), but that community need not have a future—that it have a past and a present would be enough.

3. What We Can Learn from Alvy Singer

How are we to decide whether either of these afterlife conjectures is truly plausible, or whether either Scheffler's or my speculations about the conditions or grounds for "the very idea that things matter" are correct? How, in other words, are we to proceed in constructing a theory of value (or a theory of things mattering)? Obviously, these questions are much too large to be addressed in this commentary. But as I mentioned at the beginning of my remarks, my own reflections on how we *would* respond to the doomsday scenario are inextricable from reflection on how we *should* respond. Similarly, my speculations on what the idea of value depends on are inextricable from my thoughts about what it would make rational sense for it to depend on.

In his lectures, Scheffler seems to want to resist any questions of this sort. At its most general, the question, "how would it be rational, or even reasonable, to respond to the doomsday scenario?" might well be greeted with suspicion. In the spirit of P. F. Strawson or Bernard Williams, one might reasonably be skeptical of the power and appropriateness of expecting "rationality" to help us in responding to so enormous a catastrophe as doomsday. Further, we might wonder from what perspective the question is supposed to be addressed. What assumptions about the nature and status of our values—and of their independence from an ongoing form of life—are we making insofar as we take that question to be intelligible, and why should we give those assumptions any authority? Perhaps such thoughts and concerns are behind Scheffler's resistance to talking about how we should or ought to respond to the prospect of extinction, to his determination to stick to conjectures about how we *would* respond instead and considering what these conjectures might reveal about us. Whether or not they are Scheffler's concerns, they are fair enough. Nonetheless, the question of how we should respond and that of how we would respond cannot be kept so separate as to warrant dismissing the first one entirely. For we are rational and rationality-valuing creatures, and our thoughts about what is rational, reasonable, and sensible to do and to feel affect what we ultimately decide to do and feel. If, from within the perspective of our own values, we find our initial reaction to the prospect of imminent extinction rationally unstable or mysterious, it may weaken that reaction, and if we find another reaction to be more rationally appropriate, that might move us some way toward having this other reaction.

Speaking for myself, I am moved by the question, which Scheffler explicitly dismisses, of why if imminent extinction is so catastrophic, more distant extinction is not. We know, after all, that sooner or later, the earth will be destroyed and our species will die out. When we focus on activities and projects that do not in obvious ways appear to depend on posterity for either their attainability or their point, it is hard to see why, if such projects are rendered less meaningful by the prospect of *imminent* extinction, they are not meaningless anyway, for reasons that, though available to us, we typically push from our attention.

This seems essentially to be the viewpoint of Alvy Singer. As Scheffler reminds us in Lecture 2, when the nerdy protagonist in Woody Allen's film *Annie Hall* was in grade school, his mother took him to a doctor because he was refusing to do his homework on the grounds that the universe is expanding and will someday break apart. According to Scheffler's analysis, the scene is funny not only because of Alvy's precocity but also because he takes an event so far distant in the future to be a reason not to do his homework. As Scheffler reminds us, the doctor attempts to reassure Alvy by saying that won't happen for "billions of years" (62).

As an aside, it may be worth mentioning that, even if it's true that the earth's exploding won't occur for billions of years, we can expect that our species' extinction will come much, much earlier than that. According to the biologist Ernst Mayr, the average life of a species is 100,000 years, and we have already existed about that long.[10] So, we should not expect to go on for another billion years or even another 100,000. Not even close.

But let us return to Alvy's concern and Scheffler's response. According to Scheffler, it is simply a datum that in general we do not respond to our recognition that the earth will someday be destroyed with angst or nihilism or ennui. But, he concedes, "if the universe were going to end soon after the end of his own natural life, then … Alvy might have a point" (62). I doubt that the precocious Alvy would be satisfied by this response. The fact that people *don't* get upset by the prospect of our eventual extinction does not mean that they *shouldn't*. "If I would have a point in refusing to do my homework under the doomsday scenario," Alvy might insist, "why don't I have a point anyway?" It seems to me that Alvy is within his rights, at least within the seminar room, to ask for more of an answer.

In fact, the more I think about Alvy's question (a question also asked, in essence, by Camus and Tolstoy, among others), the less confident I am that it is answerable. For if Alvy would be justified in not doing his homework if the doomsday scenario were true, this would presumably be because, as Scheffler suggests, humanity must have a future—and indeed a future of more than thirty days—if anything (that could give Alvy a reason to do his homework) is to

10. Mayr's claim is mentioned by Noam Chomsky in, among other places, his "Intelligence and the Environment," *International Socialist Review* 76 (2011), http://www.isreview.org/issues/76/feat-chomsky.shtml.

matter. But why would this be true? If the answer were that in order for anything to matter, it would have to make a *permanent* difference to the world, then Alvy's resistance to homework would be justified by the fact that the earth would explode in a billion years. If it is suggested instead that for anything to matter, it would have to make a long-lasting but *not* permanent difference (or, perhaps better, a difference to a long-lasting but not permanent community), then one might point out that from a cosmic perspective, even a billion years (much less 100,000) is not really "long-lasting."[11]

Happily, though, we can also run this puzzle the other way: If the fact that humans will eventually die out does not render dancing the tango (or walking in the woods or writing a philosophy lecture) meaningless *today*, why should the fact that we will die out in thirty or fifty or a hundred years render it meaningless either? Though I acknowledge the possibility that wish-fulfillment is distorting my reasoning powers, I have to say that I find the rational pull coming from this direction fairly persuasive. That is, since the eventual extinction of humanity does not render our current efforts at creating beauty, gaining wisdom, and helping each other valueless, neither does, or would or should, our more imminent extinction. Probably we would be initially disoriented, unsettled,

---

11. Scheffler, one may recall, speculates that the scene in the doctor's office is funny because Alvy takes an event so far in the future to be a reason not to do his homework. If, as I am imagining, Alvy's reasoning cannot be dismissed, this explanation is less plausible. Perhaps our laughter at Alvy is rather the nervous laughter of people who are made uncomfortable by being asked to acknowledge what they would prefer not to confront. Alternatively, the humor in the scene may derive from what, in the spirit of Thompson Clarke, we might put in terms of the problematic relation between the philosophical level of thought and the everyday. Woody Allen frequently exploits this relation as a source of humor. Thus, my favorite line in another of Allen's works: "What if everything is an illusion and nothing exists? In that case, I definitely overpaid for my carpet." Woody Allen, *The Complete Prose of Woody Allen* (New York: Wings Books, 1991), 10.

and depressed by the falsification of so major an assumption that we have until now taken for granted. But just as we are disoriented, unsettled, and depressed by the loss of our life's savings or the unexpected death of a loved one—or to offer a closer analogy, just as we are disoriented, unsettled, and depressed by the loss of faith in a benevolent God and a personal afterlife—we should, at least as a community, eventually, snap out of it and get back to our lives and our world. According to this line of thought, then, if we came to believe that our extinction was imminent, it would be more reasonable to resist the initial tendency to grow detached, apathetic, and depressed than to give in to it. Such reasoning, over time, ought to bring back the meaning and value to many of our activities that we initially thought doomsday would undermine.

Moreover, since the doomsday scenario is just a scenario—that is, an imaginary thought experiment—this reasoning should also bring back for us the meaning and value of the activities that would truly have been rendered pointless by imminent extinction. Now, once again, we have a reason to cure cancer, to find more sustainable energy sources, to build buildings, plant trees, repair infrastructures, and so on. Rationality, if I am right about where rationality on this topic leads, has given us our lives back, restoring the meaning and value to most, if not all, of the activities around which we previously fashioned our lives.

This might seem to deflate the point and impact of Scheffler's lectures. For, if I am right about the direction that reflection on doomsday scenarios should eventually take us, such reflection ultimately leaves everything almost where it is.[12] According to

12. I say "almost" everything because, even if I am right that the very ideas of meaning and value do not depend on humanity having a future (but only a past and a present), "The Afterlife" brings out the extent to which what is actually valuable to us does depend on humanity continuing for a good long time. As Scheffler notes, our vulnerability to the prospect of human extinction gives us more reasons to work to ensure that humanity survives than we are used to noticing (78–79).

Wittgenstein, though, this is precisely what philosophy *should* do, and he at least did not regard this as in any way deflationary. Nor should we. Scheffler has done us an invaluable service by focusing our attention on the role of posterity in our lives and in our values, and by guiding us along one plausible path toward some tentative conclusions. I take it that the jury is still out on whether that path and those conclusions are right, but the rewards of reflection on these issues and arguments seem secure, no matter how long we as a species will last.

How the Afterlife Matters

HARRY G. FRANKFURT

1.

Samuel Scheffler imagines two ways in which mankind could cease to exist. There might someday occur a global catastrophe, which would indiscriminately bring violent death to absolutely everyone. That would be the end of us. Or, with rather less commotion, a blight of infertility might spread pervasively throughout the world. That would destroy no one, but it would terminate the existence of mankind by ensuring that, while death would continue to be inescapable, no additional human beings would be born.

A variant of this second possibility would involve neither violence nor infertility but would be equally effective in eliminating the human race: suppose that abortion were freely available everywhere and that every woman, for one reason or another, chose to abort every pregnancy. My guess is that even the most committed pro-choice advocate would have serious reservations about this unlimited exercise of the right to abortion. In considering all three of these scenarios, in any case, the prospective disappearance of mankind—that is, the nonexistence of the afterlife—would seem really to bother us. We don't want it to happen. But why?

Scheffler's primary thesis in "The Afterlife" is that the afterlife "matters greatly to us [both] in its own right, and...because our confidence in the existence of an afterlife is a condition of many other things that we care about continuing to matter to us" (15). Toward the end of Lecture 2, Scheffler observes that "fiction and philosophy aside, we never have occasion to experience or to confront the reactions we would have if the destruction of human-ity were imminent. So the importance to us of the collective after-life is masked or hidden from view. We don't recognize how much it matters to us" (76).

Scheffler has now led us, both with fiction and with philosophy, into the midst of such a confrontation. In guiding our understanding and our imagination, he has been insightful and provocative. His discussion of the issues with which he has concerned himself is fresh and original. Moreover, so far as I am aware, those issues are them-selves pretty much original with him. He seems really to have raised, within a rigorously philosophical context, some new questions. At least, so far as I know, no one before has attempted to deal with those questions so systematically. So it appears that he has effectively opened up a new and promising field of philosophical inquiry. Not bad going, in a discipline to which many of the very best minds have already devoted themselves for close to three thousand years.

2.

However, in estimating how far Scheffler has actually *succeeded* in revealing "the importance to us of [a] collective afterlife [that] is masked or hidden from view," I am rather less enthusiastic. I do not believe that, in the end, he has satisfactorily assessed the status, or the role in our lives, either of the collective afterlife itself or of our normal attitudes toward it. I have no doubt that our confidence in the continuation of human history does, as Scheffler insists, play a very important—though, as he says, a "masked"—role in our lives. But I wonder whether his account of that role is quite right.

3.

Scheffler believes, as we all do, that while it may be that *many* of the things that matter to us *do* depend on our confidence in the existence of the afterlife, at least *some* of the things that now matter to us *do not*. This is only reasonable, of course, because the importance to us of some things has nothing to do with what happens or fails to happen in the future: they are important to us in virtue of what is intrinsic to them, or inherent in them, and their importance to us does not depend on anything either spatially *or temporally* outside themselves.

Scheffler mentions *comfort* and *pleasure*, and *relief from extreme pain*, as instances of what is important to us regardless of whether we believe that the afterlife exists. It is not difficult to think of other familiar instances as well—for instance, music and friendship, which are important to us for their own sakes, and from which we may derive significant value without considering, or making any assumptions at all about, whether human life will continue either beyond thirty days or beyond the current generation. The same holds for intellectual activity, which may be important to those who engage in it apart from any particular concern on their part as to whether their activity, or its product, will be of interest to anyone in the future.

Scheffler offers two examples of activities in the value of which their practitioners are likely to lose confidence "if humanity's disappearance were imminent" (53). First, "a historian...lose[s] confidence in the value of conducting his planned research on Bulgarian military history"; and second, "a political philosopher...lose[s] confidence in the value of writing additional articles" about overworked issues in political theory (54). It may be worth noticing that what is at stake in these two examples is not the same. Conducting research into an obscure subject might very well be quite rewarding to the historian, for the sheer pleasure of opening up a neglected field of study, even if no one will be interested in his results; on the other hand, writing articles is not in itself a notably satisfying activity, so the prospect of undertaking an activity that is unrewarding in itself for the sake of producing an unnecessary and probably unwelcome product is likely to be uninviting. It will probably be of no greater interest to others than an essay on the military history of Bulgaria, and it will not offer even the inherent joys of coming up with something interesting and new.

4.

I believe that Scheffler underestimates how much of what really matters to us is quite independent of our attitude toward the existence of the afterlife. He suggests that trying to find a cure for cancer would lose its importance to us if we believed that there were to be no afterlife in which people would benefit from the cure. But the challenge of solving a deep medical problem might very well lead people to work on the problem, and to consider both *solving* it and *trying* to solve it very important to them, even if the solution of the problem would actually benefit no one; thus, a person might happily try to solve chess problems, even if there were never to be anyone to admire his or her skill in doing so.

Scheffler also believes that artistic creation would tend to lose its importance to us if we lost confidence in the existence of the afterlife, because there would be no future audiences to enjoy the product of our activity. But, surely, producing a marvelous painting—or string quartet or novel—may be enormously satisfying to the artist even if there is no one, beyond the thirty days before doomsday, who will be around to appreciate and admire his or her creative work. In any event, the doomsday scenario allows the population to continue existing within those thirty days; and the infertility and abortion scenarios allow normally continuing lives for the people who comprise the final, currently alive, generation of mankind. So, regardless of what happens, so far as the afterlife is concerned, *those* people will still be around to supply appreciative audiences and grateful patients.

Some of the things that are of the greatest importance to us— such as music, friendship, and intellectual and creative activity—may be important to us quite regardless of either the existence of the afterlife or our confidence in its existence. Nevertheless, I think Scheffler *is* justified in suggesting that the importance to us of these things might then actually be less. At least, our valuing of them would very likely be *different*. They would lose that *part* of their value to us, if any, that does depend on our anticipation of the future. We would be left with that part of their value to us which is available to us when we focus just on their present reality—on appreciating their intrinsic and hence always current characteristics. Perhaps it might even be an improvement in our lives, if we concentrated our attention and our appreciation more on the value that things possess in themselves, rather than primarily on their value as means to other things.

So, a great deal of what is valuable to us, and that matters in our lives, might continue to be valuable and to matter to us even if we had *no successors* and did not think we would have any successors. Perhaps it is true that a great deal of what matters most to us would *not* do so, or perhaps it would matter to us both differently and less if the current human population had, or were expected to have, no descendants. However, *some* of the things that are very important to us might continue to be very important to us even without the existence of the afterlife and without confidence in its existence. This includes not just comfort and pleasure, of course, but whatever we value for its own sake and thus whose value to us does not depend entirely on the importance to us of something other than itself.

In fact, if we were faced with a doomsday scenario, some things might matter to us not only as much, but more than before. Faced with a global catastrophe, which would entail our own deaths, we might very well be moved to stop wasting the time left to us, and to repair certain patterns of behavior into which we had lapsed when we thought we had plenty of time left. We might be moved to care more about nourishing the intimate relationships we have with members of our family or friends. We might be moved to care more about taking a trip we had long wanted to take but had kept postponing, and so on.

In any case, it seems to me that people would not all respond in the same way to an expectation that humanity had only a brief time left. People respond differently, after all, to the expectation that they themselves have only a brief time to live. Some become morose and lose interest in practically everything that was previously important to them. Others decide to make the most of the time remaining to them, and they devote themselves to enjoying what is valuable and important to them. It seems likely to me that people would also differ in the ways in which they would confront the prospective end of all human life.

5.

Apart from questions about the afterlife concerning whether we would have human *successors* is an interesting question as to how we would be affected if we had or believed that we had no *contemporaries*. It might seem that this *should* make no difference: whatever is valuable to us for its own sake ought surely to be similarly valuable to us if we were alone in the world. This conclusion strikes me, however, as too hasty. It's true, I think, that there would still be plenty of things that *could* be important to us even if we had to confront a world altogether empty of other people. Not friendship of course, but still lots of music, as well as intellectual and creative activity, and, we must not forget, comfort and pleasure and relief from extreme pain. Those things would still possess the very same characteristics in virtue of which they are valuable to us now, but I suppose that we would be extremely lonely and that we might be seriously discouraged and depressed to the point of general immobility and of losing any genuine interest in identifying what might and what might not be important to us. Nevertheless, we could, however, in principle lead value-laden lives in a world that is both in the future and in the present empty of other people by finding importance in what we are doing or experiencing *now*, in the time that is our present without being concerned about what might or might not happen, or be happening elsewhere or in the future.

Scheffler asserts that "we need humanity to have a future if many of our own individual purposes are to matter to us now" (60). It seems to me that it is not the existence of the *afterlife*, or confidence in the future existence of humanity, that we most basically need in order for things to matter to us. Scheffler concentrates on the role of the future in making it possible for us to lead value-laden lives. But it really doesn't matter that much if there are people continuing after we die. What matters is *that there be other people, who are in some way aware of us*—whether those people exist at some point in the future or they exist right now. It is not transparent why this should be, but I believe it would be valuable to us to find out. Scheffler takes an important step in this direction, with his discussion of the limits of individualism. But he makes his point in terms of the importance to us of belonging to an ongoing human society. I believe that this is indeed important to us, but that it is only a particular part of the story. It strikes me that our experience of the world *now* is not only as important to us but also more fundamental in understanding us than our expectations of the future.

6.

Here is another point. I don't feel the force of Scheffler's suggestion that our dependence on the existence of the afterlife—or, by implication, our dependence on the contemporary existence of people—tends to undermine the widespread cynical presumption that we are incorrigibly *egoistic* creatures. As far as I can see, there is nothing particularly *altruistic* in our concern for the existence of other people now or in the future. On Scheffler's account, as it stands or as extended to cover people contemporary with ourselves—it is not *for the sake of the others* that we care about them. Manifestly, the reason we need these other people is that their existence serves our interests, not theirs—our interest in believing that our activities may be of some benefit to some others, and our interest in being appreciated.

This raises another small point about Scheffler's account of the importance to us of the existence of the afterlife—a point that is *not in conflict* with his account, but one that merely *extends* his account a little. The point is that what is important to us cannot be just that there be *other people* after we die, or even that there be *at some time* other people in addition to ourselves. What is important to us must be that there be other people *with certain particular characteristics*—for example, a susceptibility to the charms of good music and fine literature; and a readiness, when ill, to *accept* remedies that are offered by medical science, as well as a capacity on the part of at least some people *to prepare themselves* with the skills needed for applying those remedies effectively. If these characteristics were absent, the mere *existence* of the afterlife would not serve the purpose Scheffler assigns to it. We do not depend on the existence of people who are *inert* to our activities and their products.

As for the question of why we care about the existence of the afterlife—the question of why it is important to us that the human race continue to exist—I suppose that the explanation is not that we have some good reason for doing so any more than we have any good reason for caring about our own survival. In both cases, I believe, the explanation is simply Darwinian. Whatever reasons we may have or think we have for desiring to survive, or for desiring that mankind survive, it is a fact of more primary significance that natural selection has ensured that we have those desires. Scheffler also often refers to our desire to personalize our relationship to the future and to our desire to see ourselves as part of an ongoing human history. Where do these desires come from? Are we born with them, or do they arise in response to certain aspects of our cultural or social experience? Again, my view tends to be that they are versions of our instinctive desire for self-preservation, and that they are not at all specific to doomsday scenarios or to our anticipation of the end of mankind.

7.

Scheffler says that "the collective afterlife matters more to people than the personal afterlife" (72). In other words, people care more that humanity survive after they die than that they themselves survive after their own death. He points out that many people who do not believe in a personal afterlife manage nonetheless to lead quite purposeful and value-laden lives. On the other hand, as he claims to have shown, if people did not believe mankind had a future, their "ability to lead value-laden lives would be seriously eroded" (72). Thus, he concludes, "our own survival, and even the survival of those we love and care about most deeply, matters less to us than the survival of strangers, the survival of humanity itself…The prospect of the imminent disappearance of the race…poses a far greater threat to our continued ability to lead value-laden lives" (72–73).

Scheffler may be correct in maintaining that certain things would matter less if we believed the human race would soon disappear. However, as I suggested earlier, it's quite possible that, just as many people can lead value-laden lives despite believing that there is no personal afterlife, many people who expect mankind soon to disappear will be inclined to "seize the day" and enjoy the value of many things, whose importance to them does not depend upon the existence of the afterlife. So the effect on us of a loss of confidence in the afterlife may well be less dire than Scheffler supposes. Our ability to lead value-laden lives may not be as seriously eroded as he suggests. In fact, most people actually do continue to lead value-laden lives despite their recognition that, someday, in virtue of inescapable natural causes, human history truly will come to an end. We already know that someday there will be no afterlife.

It seems less clear than Scheffler supposes, then, that the existence of a collective afterlife means more to us than the existence of our own personal afterlife. For it is not at all apparent that people would be less able to lead value-laden lives if they lost confidence in the existence of the afterlife than if they lost confidence in their own personal survival. Some people, if they lost confidence in the existence of the afterlife, might indeed become too demoralized to recognize anything as important to them. But others might continue to enjoy things whose importance to them does not depend on the continuation of human history.

8.

Two final points: the first, methodological, the second, somewhat technical. Scheffler's account rests very heavily on what appear to be empirical judgments: judgments concerning what people will do, or how they are likely to respond to one or another set of circumstances. These judgments, like all empirical judgments, are susceptible to verification and empirical inquiry. In Scheffler's account, they are primarily presented for their inherent plausibility or their presumed conformity with common sense. But these only get us so far. What if empirical inquiry were to establish that these judgments were not correct? Would this require us to discard Scheffler's account wholesale, or would his account still be illuminating to us, even though it did not literally conform to reality?

The technical point is this. Scheffler asserts that valuing something consists in part in believing it to be valuable *simpliciter*. That is, I believe he must mean, believing it is valuable in itself, rather than just valuable to us. This, I believe, is a mistake. Valuing something consists, I believe, essentially in being disposed to act toward it in certain ways to sustain or enhance the viability of what is valuable in it. In the case of music, for example: not to listen to it endlessly, or encourage everyone else to listen, but to ensure its availability for listening. The question of whether the value is objective or subjective is a philosophical question, concerning which the person who does the valuing does not need to have any belief whatsoever.

Preserving the Valued or Preserving Valuing?

SEANA VALENTINE SHIFFRIN

Throughout my career, Samuel Scheffler has served as an aspirational, if unattainable, model of how to approach deep and central issues in a clear, penetrating, original, and slyly humorous way. His sharply focused work consistently offers new vantage points on themes and arguments that have been close but elusive companions, allowing them to seem fresh, new, and suddenly more tractable. These lectures provide yet another source of exactly this sort of inspiration about how to think about individualism, value, and the meaning of our lives and deaths. By doing so, they supply a vivid, sobering account of what is so horrifying about the environmental risks we have been taking and the precipice toward which we literally have been driving.

Commenting on these lectures is, although an honor, more than challenging. My dominant reaction to this work is appreciative agreement. Not only has Scheffler identified and framed a new set of philosophical questions, a welcome and precious gift in its own right, but he has argued persuasively for major, significant conclusions. In particular, I think he is right about the afterlife conjecture as well as the profound implications he draws from it, namely: First, we are far from indifferent about what happens after our deaths; this reaction is reasonable and goes deep, and this reaction confirms nonexperientialist accounts of value (15, 20). Second, in significant respects, the longevity of what else we care about reasonably matters substantially more to us than our personal longevity (26).

Reflection on this fact highlights our deeply social orientation and underscores the limits of our egoism (44).

Thus, there is little in Scheffler's account that I want directly to dispute. What I think worth exploring and fleshing out in greater detail is how exactly to characterize the way in which the present depends upon the future and what precisely constitutes the object of our shared dismay occasioned by the prospect of collective non-existence. In particular, I want to examine more closely two themes in Scheffler's lectures: First, the idea that our emotional investment in future generations derives from (or, perhaps, more weakly, exemplifies) our valuing things, projects, and activities because, as Scheffler posits, "there is something approaching a conceptual connection between valuing something and wanting it to be sustained or preserved" (22). Second, the connected idea that we are invested in a collective afterlife because of our interest in being a part of *human history* (54).

1. Conservatism about Value

I start with Scheffler's claim that conservatism about value underlies our emotional investment in the existence of future generations, where conservatism about value is the thesis that valuing something (nearly conceptually) involves wanting it to be sustained or preserved. For brevity, I will label this the "conservatism thesis." My interest in this thesis may point to a possible divide between Scheffler and myself, although I remain unsure whether there is, in fact, a fissure between our views. Many of Scheffler's examples involve individual, particular projects, their dependence on the continued participation or appreciation of future people, and the explanations these dependencies provide of the individual dismay each of us would feel at the end of collective life. I think Scheffler is right that the achievement of many (or even most) of our important particular values depends upon others yet to be. Still, I wonder whether the aggregate of those individual frustrations is what would underlie the deep and devastating *shared* dismay we would experience if the end of collective afterlife loomed. As I will argue while unpacking the conservatism thesis, I am inclined to think that the real source of the devastating, shared dismay Scheffler envisions would be triggered less by the shared condition that our disparate, particular valued projects would be frustrated and more by the prospect of the termination of the general practice of acting on reasons and of valuing.

The most plausible interpretation of the conservatism thesis probably does not involve its simplest construal, contending that for everything we value, we value its being sustained or preserved. For, it seems that there are some valuable (and valued) things that should *not* be sustained but, rather, should come to an end. Consider a beautiful musical note or a wonderful conversation. Their prolonged longevity becomes tedious or turns parodic. One may value an exquisite, artistically prepared meal, but this entails consuming it and relishing the dishes (thereby destroying them), rather than lacquering the food for posterity. To turn to a more significant example, as Bernard Williams argued in his essay "The Makropulos Case,"[1] and as Scheffler in this volume concurs on other grounds, it is good that individual human lives come to an end.[2] They may generally be too short; but not only is valuing them consistent with wanting them to come to an end, but, further, their having an end contributes to their value. That life does not persist indefinitely not only prevents it from turning sour, dull, and routine, but its having an end contributes to its significance, gives it

1. Bernard Williams, "The Makropulos Case: Reflections on the Tedium of Immortality," in *Problems of the Self: Philosophical Papers 1956–1972* (Cambridge: Cambridge University Press, 1973), 82–100.

2. Scheffler also discusses Williams's article in original and illuminating ways in Lecture 3 (88–95), coming to the same conclusion as Williams, albeit for different reasons.

poignancy, and supplies a bracing reason to organize a life around a particular set of values, making one a distinctive individual and prodding one to get on with it.

So, at least in some of these cases, it seems that I can genuinely value something, yet not want or seek to sustain or preserve it. Indeed, sometimes valuing something involves actively wanting or seeking, at the appropriate point, its end. I value the beautiful song, and the wonderful conversation, but I deliberately bring them to a close. Further, I am careful not to repeat the song too often for fear of cheapening its value, rendering it staid or clichéd. I value my life but I am with Williams and Scheffler that I would not elect to sustain it forever. (Although, assuming good health and good companions, I would not refuse an extra one hundred years or so.)

If these points hold true, they raise two related questions: First, if we put aside the simple construal of the conservatism thesis, how should we correctly understand it? Are there *some* sorts or some aspects of valuable things that are essential to preserve and sustain, such that to value them properly *is* to wish for their sustenance or preservation? Second, more specifically, does a more nuanced version of the conservatism thesis underlie our shared reaction to the prospect of the discontinuation of collective life and, if so, in virtue of what valued thing or things?

Two observations might be made on behalf of the conservatism thesis that may help us make progress in understanding its scope and assessing whether it may hold true in some cases or at some level of generality. First, in at least some of the examples I have mentioned, it may be observed that it is not so much that we resist the sustenance or preservation of the valuable thing where it is possible. Rather, in these examples, the sustenance or preservation of the valuable thing *as such* is not possible. With songs, conversations, meals, and even human lives, the valuable thing qua valuable thing cannot be indefinitely sustained *through temporal extension* because, at some point, longevity spoils or, at least, diminishes its value. In many cases, valuable events cannot be repeated, and even where they can be, frequent repetition may spoil their value (as with repeated songs and some meaningful conversations). Thus, in these cases, indefinite or extended temporal continuation (or repetition) of these valuable things is not a method of sustaining or preserving them qua valuable things.[3] Hence, they may not pose threats to the conservatism thesis if that were more narrowly drawn to claim that valuing something (nearly conceptually) involves wanting it, where possible, to be sustained or preserved qua valuable thing.

Second, there may be a better way to understand the connection between valuing and sustaining or preserving than the simple ways I have been considering. Perhaps instead of thinking only in terms of the sustaining (or preserving) of a valuable thing through temporal elongation or repetition, for some sorts of valuable things, we might regard sustaining (or preserving) as involving their occasional or regular concrete realization as well as their preservation in memory. To reformulate the conservatism thesis in a more long-winded way, we might say that valuing something involves recognizing reasons to ensure that it is somehow realized or instantiated, if it is not already, and pursued or protected to the point that it achieves and maintains something approaching its full (or perhaps

3. The right way to put this point in the case of a human life is surely more complicated. Unlike a song, the fact that it is good that a human life ends at some point does not necessarily mean that when the end comes, the end at that time is a good thing or that the life's continuation would lack value. For many human lives, their further prolongation would continue their value, even though their indefinite prolongation would not. Of course, when a life has deteriorated and become wretched, the particular end can be a good thing at the time. Even so, in such cases when the life may no longer be of value to its holder, some other indices of value may persist if the life is continued nonetheless. For example, others have obligations to treat the person and her life with respect. They might end it at her request, but they cannot take haphazard risks with it or treat its end as sport.

its distinctive) value.[4] In some cases, such as that of a piece of music, its instantiation may be relatively short. In other cases, such as the enactment of complex valuable projects, such as discovering a cure for cancer or understanding an ancient civilization, this commitment may involve multiple generations' worth of effort. Perhaps, in the case of pursuing or preserving knowledge or justice, this commitment may involve an indefinite number of generations.

Moreover, valuing something the value of which resides foundationally in its type (where the value of its token mainly derives from the value of the type) may involve wishing to sustain its *type* or *kind* in some relevant form, but not necessarily through sustaining any particular token. For example, to value a good piece of music need not necessarily involve wishing that any instance of it be sustained indefinitely, say through a feedback loop continually broadcast in a public park, but rather, to seek for it to be—at some point—fully performed (perhaps for all willing subjects of appreciation), that the music and the performance be remembered, and that on sufficiently regular occasions, there be further instantiated tokens of the type, in a form that retains its value.

This unpacking of the conservatism thesis suggests something along the following lines. There is a tight connection between valuing something and: first, registering it in (collective) consciousness or memory; and, second, where possible, seeking to instantiate it occasionally or regularly, or to sustain it over time, or both, so long as those ways achieve and retain appropriate measures of the thing's value, recognizing that the apt methods of instantiating and

---

4. Again, the point is difficult to capture precisely in the case of some complex valuable things, such as human lives, that are surely worth continuing even once they begin to decline or diminish in value to their bearers. Whereas, with other valuable things (like songs or novels), respect for their value may demand curtailing their length so that they do not persist past the apex of their value even if further appendices and additions would share some of the charm of the rest.

sustaining may differ depending on the thing in question. An interpretation of this sort has more plausibility than the simpler construal I first considered, but I remain unsure about it and unsure of the implications of my hesitation.

What continues to worry me is this: I accept and find illuminating what Scheffler says here (32–35) and in his superb essay on tradition about the ways in which sharing practices with people in the past and in the future allows us to personalize both the past and the future.[5] It may also show compassion for the investments of people in the past and represent an effort to allow their strivings to come to fruition, making their lives more meaningful in retrospect. Still, I am mindful that we cannot realize all valuable pursuits at once, temporally, or in the same social and material circumstances. The preservation and regular enactment or pursuit of the things we value, so understood, stand in some abstract tension with the invention and adoption of new valuable practices and with future generations' autonomous engagement with their lives. Some traditions, even valuable traditions, must give way if there is to be sufficient social space for new valuable practices. Indeed, some valuable new practices substantively involve not merely displacing former practices in a competition for time, space, and attention, but actively rejecting them.

Acceptance of the necessity of the displacement of the pursuit of (many) valuable practices from the past is, of course, consistent with the conservatism thesis. One may treasure the sustaining of valuable practices, while conceding that while valuable, that continuity must sometimes give way to the need and inevitability of change. Given our capacity for such wistful acceptance, however, I worry that the conservatism thesis, broadly understood, is not the source of the power behind the emotional reaction Scheffler

5. Samuel Scheffler, "The Normativity of Tradition," in *Equality and Tradition: Questions of Value in Moral and Political Theory* (New York: Oxford University Press, 2010), ch. 11, 287–311.

persuasively imagines would be provoked by the infertility scenario. I am inclined to think it is not just the termination of our particular valuable practices that would be so unsettling, but, specifically, also the conditions under which they are terminated.

Another example will help to develop the point. I rather hope there will continue to be a thriving culture of physical books with their smells, feels, and the particular sort of intellectual engagement with ideas and texts they facilitate. I am devastated by the thought of physical books disappearing for a bad reason, for example, *because* intellectualism recedes, or if the form of their loss also risked the loss of the knowledge those books have faithfully preserved. Indeed, I spend a good part of my income on keeping physical book manufacture and sales thriving. Yet, if the reason physical books become rare is that the next generations find other methods of preserving and absorbing knowledge more attractive, I find that prospect vaguely alien and wrongheaded, but it does not plunge me into despair. Larger scale examples are at hand too. If the sorts of communal values and close-knit networks of care manifested in village and small-town ways of life disintegrate because the economic pressures of globalization force massive but reluctant migration to cities, that seems terrible and tragic. Suppose instead, despite their appreciation of small-town life and for continuing a way of life in solidarity with their forebears, people nonetheless prefer the complexity, excitement, and anonymity of cities and prefer less parochial and more regular, albeit bureaucratic, methods of providing mutual social support. If it occurs for these better reasons, then the loss of small-town life seems horribly sad, but something we might reconcile ourselves to, consistent with our valuing it.[6]

6. A related, but quite differently valenced, discussion appears in G. A. Cohen, "Rescuing Conservatism: A Defense of Existing Value," in R. Jay Wallace, Rahul Kumar, and Samuel Freeman, eds., *Reasons and Recognition: Essays on the Philosophy of T. M. Scanlon* (New York: Oxford University Press, 2011), 203–30.

With respect to some valuable pursuits, their displacement by other equally valuable pursuits feels sad, sometimes wrong, but inevitable and not intolerable in the way the infertility scenario feels deeply threatening. This seems true even of projects that have not fully achieved their value; for example, the discontinuation and abandonment of a multigenerational architectural project (like Gaudí's cathedral) to make room, if necessary, instead for a public park or forest. What seems intolerable is if our valuable activity is put aside for no reason, or for a terrible reason, or if it is utterly forgotten, but not if it comes to an end so that there is room for other valuable activities to be pursued and become socially salient, or, on the other hand, to satisfy an orthogonal moral constraint.

When valuable things or activities end for no reason or for bad reasons, they inspire a special kind of dismay or despair. I posit that this despair responds to the fact that forces other than reason-based responses dictate what happens and that this fact can make our reason-oriented activity seem futile or pointless. When they end for good reasons, the change may be sad but does not seem to render our efforts to pursue appropriate reasons and values pointless.

Notably, the primary examples in the last few paragraphs involve the replacement of some valuable endeavors by others in a deliberate way that involves the ongoing practice of valuing—that is, the ongoing practice of attempting for the recognition and implementation of reasons to determine what happens to us and what we do. This suggests that one might question the degree of power that the conservatism thesis exerts with respect to specific valued things, while yet thinking it may offer grounds for profound resistance to the interruption and discontinuation of *all* valuable pursuits. Scheffler is entirely right that a more global elimination of all our specific valuable pursuits would preclude the personalization of the future that renders our individual deaths less terrifying. But that is not the point I have in mind. I have been gesturing toward the idea that it seems to matter greatly that the general practices of acknowledging value and acting on reasons continue, even if many of the particular, instantiated objects of that abstract activity alter and evolve.

Although many such projects may alter, some of our valuable projects closely tied to the general practice of valuing seem less discretionary and more mandatory. Even if the particular realizations of valuable activity acceptably alter for reasons, it also seems to matter that the general practice of *remembering* what we used to (more actively) value and how continues. Further, as Scheffler discusses, among the things we want from the collective afterlife is the sense that justice is done (67). It does not seem as though it matters that justice be done only on the condition that there happen to be future people, but also that it matters for there to be people who eventually make sufficient moral progress to get it right: to achieve justice amongst themselves and not merely conceive of it.

So, when I consider the infertility scenario, what seems devastatingly sad about it is not simply the idea that the agglomeration of particular valuable practices and pursuits we love will come to an end as such, including those projects that require multiple generations to realize them properly. What seems deeply tragic about the thought, for me, is mainly *why* they come to an end. It is not that those projects come to be disvalued for an understandable reason, because other equally valuable pursuits understandably take their place, or because we chose to stop procreating out of concern for other species or out of concern about the conditions our future children would face.[7] The tragedy is that the enactment, reenactment,

---

7. I discuss some moral issues concerning procreation in "Wrongful Life, Procreative Responsibility, and the Significance of Harm," *Legal Theory* 5 (1999): 117–48. It is an interesting, further issue whether the present generation's need for future generations to give the former's lives continued meaning provides a sufficient moral reason to create them, assuming the latter's lives would be worthwhile and assuming, as I do, that one needs a sufficient moral reason to create future people.

and recollection of valuable activities comprehensively terminate *for no adequate justificatory reason.*[8] There is an explanation, to be sure, but the termination is not caused by the implementation of a coherent reason. Moreover, unlike the end of an individual life, the fact of which contributes to the life's (full) value (assuming Williams and Scheffler are right), the fact of the termination of our collective life does not contribute to its value (108–9).[9] Finally, I am distressed by the thought that its termination in the near future entails that we will never realize a compulsory end, namely, the achievement of relations of justice and stable, ongoing, rather than sporadic, relations of moral decency.

Thus, I suggest what is *horrifying* about the infertility scenario is less the comprehensive discontinuation of the *specific* things we value, terrible as that is, and more the discontinuation of something more particular and more abstract, namely the brutal interruption and discontinuation of *valuing*—of the recognition of what matters and the undertaking of practices of enacting and realizing valuable things because we appreciate their value. If one thought that most valuable things depend for their full value upon their flourishing within a just and morally decent context, the ideas that it is crucial

8. Were there an adequate reason to end our collective lives and we took it, I think this path would render the experience less distressing but still profoundly dispiriting. I am less sure that this is only because our particular projects would be stymied (although many would be) and would not be sustained, rather than also because the universe would then consist solely of events occurring for no justificatory reason (although, at least, those events would not happen *to anyone*). Of course, it seems that in the past, the universe consisted solely of events occurring for no justificatory reason. A reason-less future seems to matter more than a reason-less past, as I go on to discuss.

9. As Scheffler observes, there are important differences between the individual and the collective case. Individuals have unified consciousnesses with attitudes (and distinctive characters). These features play a role in the argument for the good of there being an end to individual lives that would not extend to the case of collective life.

that valuing should continue and that moral relations should be achieved would then be connected.

These suggestions, in turn, connect to a particular conception of the conservatism thesis and the conditions under which it exerts strong force. I have suggested two elaborations upon the more brief articulation of the conservatism thesis with which we started. First, the tight connection is between valuing something and registering it in (collective) memory and seeking, where possible, to instantiate it occasionally or regularly or sustain it over time, or both, so long as those ways achieve and retain appropriate measures of the thing's value, *or* deliberately foregoing these forms of recognition for an appropriate justificatory reason.[10] In short, it matters that the treatment of valuable things operates according to reasons. Second, there seems to be a tight connection between the more general, abstract activity of valuing and a fervent wish that *that very* abstract activity continue, however its objects alter (for reasons) over time.

2. Human History

This proposed understanding of the conservatism thesis fuels some hesitance about what emphasis to place on the *human* aspect of Scheffler's remark that "the actual value of our activities depends on their place in an ongoing human history" (54). Just as what may ultimately matter deeply is not that *my* or *our* current valued practices continue, but that valuing for good reasons continues, so it may not ultimately matter deeply that *human-led* valuing practices continue, rather than valuing practices by rational agents. Suppose humans were to die out, like the Neanderthals, because we succumbed to evolutionary pressures but that another rational

10. I am skeptical, though, that there could be an adequate justificatory reason for not registering in collective memory in some way the people who lived and the things they valued.

species emerged and thrived in our stead. Suppose further that subsequent rational species remembered us fairly accurately, recognized our value, appreciated what we valued and why, strived to behave morally, and carried on engaging in valuable practices for reasons, though largely different practices. For me, it is a bizarre and humbling future to contemplate, but not a profoundly depressing one. It matters that valuing for reasons does not end abruptly—for no reason—and that the practice of history—that is, of remembering who existed and understanding what they valued—continues. I am less sure that it centrally matters that remembering and valuing is done by creatures like us.

I will conclude with a somewhat related question about the significance of being part of a *history* with a collective past and a collective future as opposed to the significance of being part of a collective with a future. Lucretius observed that we are untroubled about our prenatal nonexistence relative to our anguish over our personal postmortem nonexistence.[11] He thought that our indifference toward our prenatal nonexistence should render us less concerned about our own mortality. Most have been unmoved by that suggestion, but acknowledge the asymmetry and take it to provide an interesting puzzle.

In that light, it is tempting to ask whether there is a similar asymmetry with respect to collective prehistory and collective extinction. Of course, unlike our prenatal nonexistence, our collective life did preexist each of us for a long stretch. But, at one point, humans did not exist and, with fortune (and environmental reforms), our collective nonexistence will be longer off than our individual mortality.

I think that something like the Lucretian attitudinal asymmetry does exist with respect to our collective lives. First, in contrast to the

11. Lucretius, *De Rerum Natura*, III., 830–4z, trans. A. A. Long and D. N. Sedley, *The Hellenistic Philosophers* (Cambridge: Cambridge University Press, 1987), vol. 1, 151–52.

eventual prospect of the end of the collective afterlife, our prior collective nonexistence is less a source of distress and despair than a source of interest and wonder. When we did not exist, many valuable things were not recognized or deliberately enacted. There may have been compassion, play, lower mathematics, and song among the animals once they came along, but there was no literature, architecture, painting, philosophy, higher mathematics, and so forth; some of those animals may have valued each other and the environment, but the sort of complex, self-conscious valuing we are capable of was probably absent. Those absences seem unproblematic. Yet, a future without valuing feels desolate in a way that, if we focus on it, may directly affect our lives and upset our equanimity.

Perhaps that is because our prior collective nonexistence was so long ago. Perhaps a collective nonexistence comparably far out in the future should not trouble us, though it would understandably upset those closer to it. But suppose our beginnings were more abrupt and closer in temporal proximity. Suppose we discovered that some ludicrous science-fiction conspiracy story was true— something like the Scientology myth[12]—but occurring much more recently. Very different aliens created us and deposited us here, around 150 years ago, left misleading evidence and implanted effective but false myths about our personal, social, and biological histories. Let's imagine that the personalities and fake histories they manufactured didn't represent their values or a conscious enactment of a normative alternative; perhaps our profile was just the output of a fancy randomized simulation game. In any case, don't

12. See, e.g., Bent Corydon and L. Ron Hubbard Jr., *L. Ron Hubbard, Messiah or Madman?* (Secaucus, NJ: Lyle Stuart, 1987) (describing the Scientology account of the alien creation of clusters of "Thetans," the implanted brainwashing to which Thetans were subject, and the ongoing but hidden embeddedness of Thetan clusters in our minds), 360–66; Joel Sappell and Robert Welkos, "Scientologists Block Access to Secret Documents, 1,500 Crowd Into Courthouse to Protect Materials on Fundamental Beliefs," *Los Angeles Times*, November 5, 1985, 1.

imagine the case as one in which we share an unknown normative continuity with the aliens. Aside from our distress at the deception, our serious misapprehensions about our past, and our concern about the existence of manipulative aliens, would the fact that human history more recently did not exist be *as upsetting* as the prospect of collective nonexistence within 150 years?

Despite my own introduction of the case, I find it hard to wrap my mind around that sort of science fiction. It's hard to invent the right case. I concede it is especially hard to shake off the issues about deception, self-ignorance, reorientation, fear, and betrayal. The scenario would surely be distressing but, I think, mainly for those reasons. For those whose identities and projects revolve around continuing and preserving historical traditions, their practices of valuing would surely become unhinged. But, for others, I suspect the distressing feature of the situation would not center on the fact that we would be without much of a collective past. If one somehow put those other issues aside, the fact that we lacked a true collective history, I think, would not be *as* distressing as the lack of a collective future. If so, the Lucretian asymmetry holds true of both individuals and the collective, and its appearance is not attributable merely to the far distance of our collective nonexistence and the difficulty of imagining it.[13]

Because there was a human past, it seems important (as Scheffler discusses in his work on tradition) to share some things and practices with the people from before—to know about them, recognize them, and enact some of the same practices to share activity, if not time and space, with them.[14] But were we pioneers, starting virtually from the beginning, I am less confident that the absence of a rich history would matter as much as the absence of a rich collective

13. I suspect that this asymmetry is related to another: the fact that our prior injustice rankles less than the prospect of our future injustice. Whether related or not, the latter asymmetry is surely easier to think about.

14. Scheffler, "The Normativity of Tradition," in *Equality and Tradition*.

afterlife that involves a continuation of the practices of valuing, if not the continuation of our actual values. History matters most if there is a history, whereas, as Scheffler remarks, the afterlife matters whether there will be one or not (55).

This also suggests that part of what matters most is not simply being a part of human (or rational) history and sustaining value through time, but doing so in a particular future-directed way— being a part of a project that, now that it is under way, makes progress and develops according to reasons.[15] Although I am unsure whether Scheffler would agree, I have been suggesting that *that* project, at bottom, should be abstractly identified as the project of responding to reasons and values appropriately, although each of us does our individual part by endorsing and pursuing specific values and thereby becoming distinctive individuals with fully valuable lives.

15. In saying there is a sense in which our valuing is future directed, I do not mean to deny or diminish the importance of nonetheless evincing a backward-looking concern for our predecessors and helping, where feasible, to achieve some of the projects that make their lives more meaningful in retrospect.

That I Should Die and Others Live

NIKO KOLODNY

1.

In Lecture 3, Samuel Scheffler argues for two main theses, alternately unsettling and reconciling:

A. We have reason to fear death, independently of its "depriving" us of the goods of future life, because it "extinguishes" us: brings it about that we no longer exist. (My terms.)

B. If we never died, we would not live (stronger conclusion) a life at all, or (weaker conclusion) a value-laden life.

From B, Scheffler draws, or seems to draw, two conclusions:

C. Never dying but still living a life, or never dying but still living a value-laden life, is conceptually incoherent.

D. Never dying would be a disaster for us, since it would deprive us of a life, or of a value-laden life.

I take it that C does *not* mean that it is incoherent that we should never die, period: that our organism continues in its vital functions, including support of consciousness, indefinitely. Never dying is at least conceptually possible.

I begin by drawing out the rather striking implications of A. Scheffler more or less explicitly accepts one of these:

    E. One can have reason to fear something to which there is no possible alternative—in some sense of "possible" stronger than conceptually possible, but still quite weak.

But there are others.

Observe that death might not be depriving for a person who is unfortunate enough: the evils of future life for that person might outweigh the goods. According to A, such an unfortunate still has an "egoistic" reason to fear death: extinction.[1] Perhaps this is so. Nevertheless, it seems to me that such an unfortunate has no egoistic reason to *avoid* death. I rest this conclusion not on any sophisticated metaphysics, but instead simply on imaginative entry into the unfortunate's deliberative situation. If the evils in prospect outweigh the goods, then that, to my mind, settles the question (ignoring, of course, nonegoistic effects on others, or other things of value, including, perhaps, disrespect for the value of personhood itself). It is not as though the "bad of extinction" puts a finger on the scales in favor of continued life that some further net deficit in the goods of continued life must outweigh. Indeed, there seems something misplaced, a kind of category mistake, in the thought that extinction itself is the sort of thing that could be weighed against the goods and bads that a life might contain.

    This suggests:

    F. There is no egoistic reason to avoid extinction as such.[2]

    1. However, Scheffler seems to suggest at points that fear of death depends on deprivation: "assuming that they are glad to be alive and would like to go on living" (102), "our fear testifies to the depth of our confidence in the value of all that death brings to an end" (110), and, possibly, "*unwanted* cessation of one's existence" (103, my emphasis).

    2. More metaphysical routes to F and J below have been suggested. They turn on the claim that one does not exist at the time of the misfortune of death, or, at any rate, cannot experience it. For a contemporary example, see Stephen Rosenbaum, "How to Be Dead and Not Care: A Defense of Epicurus," *American Philosophical Quarterly* 23, no. 2 (1986): 217–25. (Indeed, the claims are

A and D imply, not all that surprisingly:

G. One can have reason for egoistic fear of something that one has overwhelming egoistic reason *not* to avoid.

Going to the dentist, as Scheffler says, is a familiar example of this. But A and F imply, more surprisingly:

H. One can have reason for egoistic fear of something that one has *no* egoistic reason to avoid.[3]

It is harder to think of other examples of H. There is *some* reason to avoid dental appointments. They are unpleasant.

If we assume:

I. If something would be in some way bad for one, then one has egoistic reason to avoid it,

then Scheffler may also be committed to:

J. One can have reason for egoistic fear of something that is in no way bad for one.[4]

Another route to J, owing to Lucretius, appeals to the apparent symmetry between prenatal and postmortem nonexistence.

---

sometimes taken to support the stronger conclusions that, even supposing that future life promises more good than bad, one has no reason to avoid death, and it is not bad for one.) I don't rely on such claims here.

3. One might reply that, *as things are*, no one can *avoid* extinction. We can only *postpone* it. And we often have reason to fear things that we have no reason to postpone (e.g., dental surgery, which will be as painful whenever it occurs). There is nothing surprising about that. But we are assuming that it is at least conceptually possible that things are different: that the unfortunates *could* avoid extinction. It seems, even in that case, that they would have no reason to avoid it.

4. In passing, Scheffler entertains this possibility, when he observes that denying the Second Epicurean Conclusion may not require denying the First Epicurean Conclusion (84–85).

1. One's prenatal nonexistence as such—that is, apart from depriving one of the goods of a longer life[5]—was in no way bad for one.

2. There is no relevant difference, in this context, between prenatal nonexistence as such and postmortem nonexistence as such.

3. Therefore, one's postmortem nonexistence as such will be in no way bad for one.

If J is false, that is, if:

4. One has egoistic reason to fear only what will be in some way bad for one,

then it would follow that A is false; that is:

5. One has no egoistic reason to fear one's postmortem nonexistence.

So Scheffler may be committed, in another way, to J. He may need J to block this argument against A.

Note further that:

6. If X is a past event or condition, such that, were an event or condition, Y, relevantly similar to X to lie in the future, one would reasonably fear Y, it is reasonable for one to feel a sense of disquiet in contemplating X.

---

5. There is also a puzzle of this kind surrounding the depriving effects of death. Why is one's not being born earlier not as much of a misfortune as one's not dying later, given that they both deprive one of goods of additional life? But we are setting deprivation aside. For attempts to solve this puzzle, see Thomas Nagel, "Death," in *Mortal Questions* (Cambridge: Cambridge University Press, 1979), 1–10; Fred Feldman, "Some Puzzles About the Evil of Death," *Philosophical Review* 100, no. 2 (1991): 205–27; Frederick Kaufman, "Pre-Vital and Post-Mortem Non-Existence," *American Philosophical Quarterly* 36, no. 1 (1999): 1–19; and Anthony Brueckner and John Fischer, "Why Is Death Bad?" *Philosophical Studies* 50 (1986): 213–23.

For example, someone who barely escaped an atrocity, or experienced the horror of war, cannot reasonably be expected to contemplate those past events with equanimity, even if he knows full well that they will never return. Indeed, one imagines that he would shudder at the thought of it. But I take it that:

7. It is not reasonable for one to feel disquiet in contemplating one's prenatal nonexistence as such.

Whatever disquiet I might feel at thoughts of Nixon's first term, it would be bizarre for me to feel disquiet about the fact that, during it, I did not yet exist. But 2, 6, and 7 also imply that Scheffler's A is false. So perhaps Scheffler must deny 6 too:

K. It may not be reasonable for one to feel disquiet about X, even if X is a past event or condition, such that, were an event or condition, Y, relevantly similar to X to lie in the future, one would reasonably fear Y.

Scheffler might seek to avoid J and K in another way. I have been supposing that what we fear, in fearing extinction, is the "state" of postmortem nonexistence. This makes 2—the claim that prenatal and postmortem nonexistence are relevantly similar—relevant. But perhaps what we fear is, specifically, the "passage" *into* this state of nonexistence.[6] And perhaps the passage *into* the state of nonexistence—the passage that death involves—is unlike the passage *out* of it—the passage that birth (or gestation or postnatal development) involves. But, if so, what is it about the *passage* into nonexistence that we fear, apart from the fact that, its having taken place, we will "be" in a *state* of nonexistence? And how is it different from the passage *out* of nonexistence, which can seem no less "uncanny" or "impossible" (86)?[7]

---

6. Indeed, Scheffler tends to characterize the object of fear in terms of the "transition" into nonexistence: "will simply stop being," "is now going to end" (86), "will cease to exist" (102), and "cessation" (103).

7. The "temporal asymmetry" described by Derek Parfit, *Reasons and Persons* (Oxford: Oxford University Press, 1984), sect. 67—that we are not as upset

If A indeed implies H, J, and K, this fact need not refute A. It may only testify to something that Scheffler is at pains to emphasize: the singularity of our fear of death. Insofar as it is not fear of the deprivation of the goods of further life, our fear of death may be, unlike any other fear, a fear of something that we have no reason to avoid, something that is in no way bad for us, and something whose analogue in the past gives us not the slightest disquiet to contemplate.

2.

I now turn to the implications of C and D. Scheffler notes that C implies:

L. The wish that our lives, or value-laden lives, should go on forever is a wish for something conceptually incoherent (100).

What, if anything, follows from this? Does it follow that the wish is unreasonable? We can reasonably have wishes for distinct objects that we know are not compossible. Is it so obvious that we cannot also reasonably wish for their impossible combination? Perhaps the reply is that there is no such wish, reasonable or otherwise. As described, there is no propositional object for it to have.

But, still, does it follow that it is unreasonable to *regret* the very fact of C: that our lives, or our lives if they are to be value-laden, must come to an end? That attitude has a propositional object: a

by news of *past* egoistic bads as we are by news of *future* egoistic bads—might be invoked as a theory of error for claim 1, which would alleviate one source of pressure to accept J. It only seems that prenatal nonexistence is in no way bad for us, the error theory would say, because it lies in the past. But this would not make K less puzzling. Why do we not contemplate our prenatal nonexistence with horror, whereas we fear its future equivalent, postmortem nonexistence, even though we *do* generally contemplate with disquiet past events and conditions whose future equivalents we greatly fear?

necessary truth. It might be replied that we can reasonably *regret* something only if there is a conceptually possible alternative to it. But can Scheffler give this reply? As noted earlier, he accepts E: that we can reasonably *fear* our death, even though, in a still very weak sense of "possible," there is no possible alternative.

At any rate, according to C, the desire for worthwhile eternal life is for something conceptually impossible (and so perhaps no desire at all), and, according to D, the desire never to die is for something that would be a disaster for us, depriving us of a meaningful life or even any life at all. Yet, as Scheffler notes, the desire never to die and, moreover, to enjoy eternal life seems widespread (65–66) (even when distinguished from other desires that might fuel yearning for a personal afterlife, such as being connected with loved ones or seeing justice done [66–68]). Romans 6:23 did not, and still does not, fall on deaf ears. What are we to make of this?

One possibility, short of attributing to such people an even deeper confusion, is suggested by the fact that knowing that we would never die would, as Scheffler notes (68), relieve us of the fear of death. Indeed, if Scheffler's A is correct—if we have reason to fear our extinction as such, whenever it should occur—then it is the only *rational* way to relieve us of that fear. Unless our extinction will *never* occur, the reason for fear is still present. Assuming that, in general, we have reason to want to vacate reasons for fear, as such, we have at least that reason to wish never to die.

Another possibility, again short of attributing to such people an even deeper confusion, is that they really desire not infinite time, but more time. That is, for any time that they might die, they desire that they should die, but later than that. This seems a reasonable structure of desires. *Whenever* we die, our dying *then* would be *all things considered worse for us than dying later* (at least if our lives are worth living). First, it would be worse in one respect: it would deprive us of the goods that we would have enjoyed had we had a longer but finite life. Second, it would be *no better* in another respect: our dying then is no better than dying later for bringing it about that we die at some point, and so for avoiding the catastrophe of immortality.

This may also ease an apparent tension between C and D, on the one hand, and the "conservative" impulse (22–23, 35), on the other hand. Suppose that the impulse is interpreted as: to value something is to wish, or think it good, or see oneself as having reasons to strive, that it last forever. Then to value our lives is, perversely, to think good, and so on, something that is conceptually impossible or a disaster for us: that our lives last forever. But suppose the impulse is interpreted as: to value something is, with respect to any particular time it might end, to wish for, think it good and so on, that it not end until later. That structure of desire is, as far as I can tell, coherent.

3.

Next, the case for B. Why should we accept B, and so C and D: that if our lives were to go on forever, they would not be value laden or lives at all? One possible reason is that *no* life that went on forever would be a life, or a value-laden life. But why accept that?

Scheffler offers three kinds of reasons. He suggests, first, that a life, or value-laden life, requires a *progression through stages, change, development*, and so on (96).

But an infinite life could involve a progression through stages, even a progression through (an infinite number of) finite stages. Compare the progress of humanity. It seems intelligible that humanity should go on forever, but that doesn't obviously mean that humanity would not progress, change, develop, and so on.

He suggests, second, that a life, or value-laden life, requires, or requires the possibility of, *loss, illness, injury, harm, risk, and danger*. And these, in turn, draw much of their content from the possibility of death (96–97).

But much of their content, it seems to me, would remain without the possibility of death. There could still be the possibility of loss of honor, reputation, self-respect, good conscience; failing in one's projects; hurting, disappointing, being separated from, rejected by those one cares about; being tyrannized, enslaved, humiliated by others; losing skills, capacities, control over one's body or environment; as well as pain and suffering.

Indeed, one might think that immortality would raise the stakes to terrifying heights. Having done what one can't live with oneself for doing is bad enough—but, despite that, having to live with oneself for eternity? Suffering a fate worse than death is bad enough—but suffering such a fate with no hope of the relief of death? Surely much of the power of the myths of the punishments of Prometheus and Sisyphus, and of depictions of hell, owes to their images of *unending* torment. Far from immortality removing risk, danger, and so forth, the thought would instead be that immortality would make risk and danger paralyzing or crushing. (Admittedly, this might be a route to a *different* conclusion to the effect that mortality has some redeeming feature: not that mortality makes things matter, but that it keeps them from mattering oppressively much.)

A third reason Scheffler gives is that *temporal scarcity is a necessary, or otherwise important, condition for valuing*. He argues, very suggestively, that we could scarcely so much as make sense of structured deliberation, of the need to make comparative evaluations and so, arguably, evaluations at all, in its absence (99).

But why couldn't other kinds of scarcity serve much the same function? It doesn't follow from the fact that *time* is not scarce that *nothing* is.

In any event, there could still be temporal scarcity even if time alive was not scarce. Scheffler notes that there might be limited time to engage with perishing objects, or nonrepeating events (90 n. 15). But there would be many other sources of temporal scarcity. (1) If an immortal life would be made of finite developmental stages, then the finitude of those stages would make for temporal scarcity. Regrets for missed opportunities in one stage might be carried into the next stage of life. (George Bernard Shaw's quip comes to mind, about how youth is wasted on the young.) (2) Imagine an immortal life where our time with others was limited: that you would eventually be separated from those you had come to love, albeit not by death. (3) Some goods are intrinsically temporally "positional" or depend on "timing." To discover or invent something, you have to be the *first*. To have a monogamous marriage to someone, you need to get your marriage proposal accepted by her *before* someone else does. (4) In general, in competition for scarce goods, "getting there before the other guy" is of paramount importance (especially so, one might think, if the alternative is *eternal* deprivation).

Finally, I'm struck by the fact that small children seem to care about many things—such as the attention of their parents, control over their environment, the acquisition of new skills—often quite intensely, even though they don't have much grasp of mortality, especially not of their own. Of course, one might attribute to them greater implicit sophistication in their beliefs about mortality or less sophistication in their alleged valuing. But if we take my description at face value, then it suggests that, even if awareness of scarcity, or even of temporal scarcity, is necessary for valuing, such awareness induced by awareness of one's own mortality is not.

I have been raising questions about the thesis:

> If we never died, we would not live a life, or a value-laden life, *because no life* that went on forever would be a life, or a value-laden life.

A weaker thesis, easier to defend, is:

> M. If we never died, we would not live a *human* life, or a life laden with *human* values, because no life that went on forever would be a *human* life, or a *human* value-laden life.[8]

Yet M may read like "merely a trivial truth resting on a stipulative definition" (100). It doesn't rule out the possibility of a *different*

---

8. Indeed, the qualification "human" appears throughout Scheffler's discussion.

kind of eternal life, or an eternal life with *different kinds* of values. Why should one care that that eternal life, or its values, wouldn't be classified as "human"? Is it so foreign to yearning for immortality, after all, to chafe at being confined to the merely human?

Perhaps the reply is that what matters is not that those values wouldn't meet certain criteria of "humanness" per se, but instead something that this implies: namely, that (on the assumption that our actual values *do* meet these criteria for humanness) those values would simply not be *our* values. "At best," the thought would run, "a life that went on forever would be laden with values very different from our values: the values to which we have become attached and by which we have come to be defined—under the lengthening shadow of our mortality. Perhaps we could wish eternal life for homo sapiens who have not yet become attached to values such as ours. But could we reasonably wish it for ourselves? Imagine that we were given, here and now, the option of eternal life. This would be, we are assuming, the option of a life estranged from *our* values. Setting aside the question of whether we could see this life as one that *we*, rather than some stranger, would go on to lead, how could we, who value *our* values, value *it*? To be puzzled about why we shouldn't value this different, everlasting life would be like being puzzled about why I shouldn't trade in the man or woman I love for a substitute with better actuarial prospects."

Note that, on this line of thought, we need not deny that whatever values might be available to us were we never to die would be classifiably "human." We might observe merely that, even so, they would not be the *particular* human values to which we are *actually* attached. This line of thought would rest on an even weaker thesis:

N. The lives that we are now in the midst of leading could not continue to be laden with the *values that they actually are* were we never to die, because *those* values presuppose our death.

Whether N is defensible is another question. But it seems much easier to defend than B. And this retrenchment would seem to meet

Scheffler's objective just as well. Or, more guardedly, and assuming nothing about anyone's "objectives," the emotional and practical import for us of N might differ little from that of B. For, while we would not be forced to the stronger conclusion that mortality is necessary for a value-laden life, or even for a human value-laden life, we would be forced to the weaker conclusion that *our* mortality is necessary for *our* life being laden with *our* values. And given that *our* life is the one up to us to lead, and that we *actually do* value our values, the upshot seems all the same *for us*.

4.

If I have more reservations than Scheffler about his claims in Lecture 3, I suspect that I have *fewer* than he has about his claims in "The Afterlife." That is, I suspect that I am willing to take his conclusions further than he is prepared to.

Scheffler qualifies, or guards against a misunderstanding of, his claim about what the afterlife conjecture reveals about the limits of our egoism. He seems to say (77–78) that:

O. Although our *equanimity* is more dependent on beliefs about the survival of humanity than our own individual survival, we aren't necessarily more *motivated* to ensure the survival of humanity than our own survival.

O might be taken to suggest a distinction between motivation and affect, as two "ways in which we might be said to care." The point, then, would be to warn the reader that the afterlife conjecture may not show that we are *more motivated* to ensure the survival of humanity than we are to ensure our own personal survival.

For two reasons, I wondered about this. First, it seems to follow more or less directly from Scheffler's earlier claims—that the afterlife matters to us very much and that mattering to us is, in part, a matter of being motivated (16–17)—that we are in fact very motivated to ensure the survival of humanity. Or, at least, if this is not the case, then it would seem to call for some special explanation. Why, when it comes to the afterlife, is mattering only an affective, rather than motivational, affair, whereas in the other cases Scheffler describes, they go together?

Second, it seems to me independently very plausible that we *are* highly motivated, in a suitably conditional sense, to ensure the survival of humanity. Granted, we don't do a lot to ensure the survival of humanity, whereas we do a lot to ensure our own survival (visit the doctor, fasten seatbelts, and so on). But I suspect that this is because we don't see the survival of humanity as being seriously threatened (perhaps precisely because, for the reasons Scheffler gives, mass extinction is too horrible to contemplate, despite mounting evidence of the threats), because there is less that we can do as individuals about it, because we expect that others will step in to do it for us, because even if we slack off today there will still be time to set things right tomorrow, and so on. When confronted with a clear-cut case, in which we knew that it was up to us, it strikes me as very plausible that we would want to die prematurely, if this would mean that humanity survived.

Scheffler asks us to consider the following choice:

Option A: I die prematurely, but humanity survives long after I am gone.
Option B: I live to a ripe old age, but humanity perishes when, in Option A, I would have died.

He observes that you don't need to be particularly altruistic to choose Option A. However, he also observes that this case tells us less about limits to our egoism than about limits to our individualism, or simply to our capacity for enduring loneliness. For many of us, being deprived of all human contact would be a fate worse than death. And this deprivation might be equally bad for us even if it occurred not by the extinction of everyone else, but instead by our being separated from them forever, by being shot into space.

But consider a different choice:

> Option A: I die prematurely, but humanity survives long after I am gone.
>
> Option C: I live to a ripe old age, but humanity perishes when, in this Option, I die.

I don't think you need to be a particularly altruistic person either to be motivated to choose Option A over Option C. You just need to share the sense, brought to articulacy by Scheffler's discussion, that your life in Option C would lack much of the value and meaning that it would have under Option A, because of the dependence of that value and meaning on the collective afterlife.

By "motivated to choose X," I don't mean: "necessarily able to bring oneself to choose X if given the opportunity." It wouldn't be easy voluntarily to give up one's life, even when the meaning of one's life depended on it, just as it isn't easy voluntarily to saw off a gangrenous limb, even when one's life depends on it. But I don't think that's the relevant sense of "motivated to choose." I mean instead—as seems consonant with Scheffler's use of "motivated" (17)—that we would (sincerely and without needing special argument) see ourselves as having stronger reasons to choose it if given the opportunity. And I suspect that many of us, even those of us who are quite selfish by ordinary measures, would see ourselves as having such reasons, even if we might, incontinently, fail to follow them where they lead.

So I wonder whether the real distinction is not O, which contrasts affect with motivation, but instead something more like:

> P. Although we may in fact care (in both ways, not just affectively but also motivationally) more about the survival of humanity than our own survival, our *grounds* for caring are, in a recognizable sense, more *egoistic* than *altruistic*.

That is, while we are concerned with the survival of humanity, this is not because, at root, we have disinterested concern for future people in themselves, but instead because their existence is a necessary condition of many objects of broadly egoistic concern: the value of *our* pursuits, *our* enjoying simple pleasures, and so on. Although it isn't quite right, one might try to bring out the egoism by saying that we value future people as "means." It's just that the afterlife conjecture shows that future people are much more essential means than we might have thought. As Scheffler says, we are more dependent on them than we may realize.

Reply to Commentators

SAMUEL SCHEFFLER

Death, Value, and the Afterlife: Responses

It is a rare privilege to have one's work given such close attention by such a distinguished group of philosophers. I am grateful to all four discussants for their generous remarks and thoughtful challenges. I cannot do justice here to all the points they have raised. I will try to respond to their major criticisms and to use the opportunity afforded by those criticisms to clarify and expand on certain themes of the lectures. I'm afraid that, in the nature of the case, the enterprise of responding to one's critics makes it almost impossible to avoid a certain defensive posture. This is especially regrettable in this instance, because, as is all too obvious, my lectures do not develop a carefully worked-out theory nor do they purport to be the final word on the issues they address. The lectures are exploratory and speculative, and I am particularly grateful to the discussants for their willingness to enter into the spirit of the lectures and to offer their own ideas about the issues and questions that I have raised. Their many acute observations and insights point the way toward further investigation of those issues.

The Limits of Egoism

Susan Wolf is not persuaded that the afterlife conjecture, even if true, shows anything significant about the limits of our egoism. In thinking about her skepticism, it is important to keep in mind that there are different things that might be meant by describing someone as an egoist and, correspondingly, different things that might be meant in speaking about the limits of a person's egoism. For example, in saying that a person is an egoist, one might be saying something about the content of the person's goals, aims, and aspirations. Roughly, one might mean that the person's aims are largely or exclusively focused on himself or on his own satisfaction or gratification. Another thing one might mean in saying that a person is an egoist is, again roughly, that the person's emotions are never or almost never directly affected by what happens to other people. The person is simply unconcerned with what happens to others. What is at stake here is not the content of the egoist's aims but his susceptibility to being affected by the fortunes and misfortunes of others.

When I spoke of the limits of our egoism, it was the second of these two things that I had in mind. I meant that reflection on the doomsday and infertility scenarios shows that we are more vulnerable to the misfortunes of others than we may have realized. So when Wolf provisionally suggests that even people who strike us as quintessential egoists might lose interest in their activities when faced with one of those scenarios, I take this conjecture to support my position. She also says, however, that this would not show these people or their interests to be any less egoistic than they initially appeared. I agree that it would not show them to be less egoistic in the first of the two respects I mentioned. Even if one of Wolf's quintessential egoists would lose interest in his activities in the face of the infertility scenario, that doesn't make his current projects any less egoistic in their content. Still, it does show something about the extent to which he is egoistic in the second of the respects that I mentioned. It means that the strength and character of his motivations, the content of his emotions and his beliefs about what is worth doing, and his capacity to engage with enthusiasm in his own projects are all highly sensitive to the fates of human beings— or possible human beings—other than himself and his intimates. The fact that even quintessential egoists would be demoralized or even devastated by the nonexistence of future people means that they are vulnerable to and dependent on others in unexpected ways. And I take these forms of vulnerability and dependence to show something significant not only about the nature but also about the limits of their egoism—and of ours—despite the obvious respects in which the content of their current projects and aims remains egoistic.

But don't our very vulnerability and dependence demonstrate that there is a sense in which our concern for the existence of future people is egoistic? Harry Frankfurt argues, in this spirit, that even if our reactions to the doomsday and infertility scenarios reveal the extent of our vulnerability to others, there is nothing altruistic about those reactions. Instead, what they reveal is the extent to which the existence of future people serves our own interests.

Egoism understood as a matter of emotional invulnerability to the fates of others may be distinguished not only from egoism in the content of one's aims and goals but also from egoism as a motivational trait involving, roughly, an overriding determination to ensure one's own survival and well-being. In "The Afterlife," I drew on this second distinction when I proposed two different ways of interpreting the claim that the afterlife conjecture reveals limits to our egoism. According to the first interpretation, the claim is that we are more dependent on others than we often suppose, particularly with respect to our ability to lead lives of value. According to the second interpretation, the claim is that we are more highly motivated to ensure the survival of others than to ensure our own survival. I emphasized that I was making only the first of these claims. I also said that, even though I do think there are some contexts in which we might be more highly motivated to ensure the survival of others than to ensure our own, the reasons for this were not particularly altruistic. But Frankfurt's suggestion is, in effect, that even our dependence on others has an egoistic basis. Niko Kolodny agrees. On the one hand, Kolodny thinks that I should have gone further than I did in defending the second, motivational claim. He believes that we "*are* highly motivated, in a suitably conditional sense, to ensure the survival of humanity" (171). He offers some interesting speculations as to why, as things now stand, we don't appear to act on this motivation very often, and he provides strong reasons for thinking that, nevertheless, our concern about the future of humanity is not merely affective but is also motivational. On the other hand, Kolodny, like Frankfurt, thinks my own arguments reveal that the grounds of this concern are, in a recognizable sense, more egoistic than altruistic. After all, we are concerned about the survival of humanity because the existence of future people is a necessary condition for *our* leading value-laden lives. So if in one way our dependence on them reveals the limits of our egoism, in another way it reveals the extent of our egoism: we depend on them if *we* are to lead value-laden lives.

I don't have any significant substantive disagreement with this. Indeed, it was my intention to emphasize how much we depend on the survival of others. However, I don't find the use of the term "egoism" particularly helpful in making this point. It does not enhance, and may in fact inhibit, our appreciation of the ways in which our lives are intertwined with the lives of others and the ways in which our attitudes and motivations are affected by the fates of others. Once we have called attention to the ways in which the existence of future people matters to us and the ways in which we are dependent on the survival of humanity, describing these things as manifestations of egoism adds nothing and is likely only to mislead. Consider an analogy. We do not label as egoistic the grief that a mourner feels at the loss of a loved one, even if the mourner's grief is in large part a response to what *he himself* has lost. Nor do we classify the mourner's reaction as altruistic, of course. The point is rather that we do not have recourse to the vocabulary of egoism and altruism here at all. In general, the use of that vocabulary does little to illuminate the attitudinal reactions through which people register the extent of their dependence on, vulnerability to, and entanglement with other people and their fates.

But then shouldn't I have refrained from using the term "egoism" myself? If it is misleading to describe our dependence on others as a *manifestation* of egoism, then isn't it also misleading to claim, as I did, that our dependence reveals the *limits* of our egoism? These are fair questions. It did seem to me when I wrote "The Afterlife" that it was natural to describe our reactions to the doomsday and infertility scenarios as revealing some limits of our egoism, where by "egoism" I had in mind our self-sufficiency and invulnerability to the fates of others. And I confess that it still seems more natural to me to speak this way than it does to describe our very dependence on others as a manifestation of egoism.[1] But nothing turns on a word. In the end, what is important is simply to appreciate the complex and varied ways in which we depend on others, including those who do not yet exist.

Afterlife Conjectures

So far I have discussed the commentators' doubts about whether the afterlife conjecture, if true, shows anything significant about the limits of our egoism. Both Frankfurt and Wolf also express forceful reservations about the truth of the conjecture, although neither of them flatly rejects it and both seem to think that it is at least partly correct. Some of their doubts concern the range of activities whose perceived value would be jeopardized by the imminent extinction of the human race. Each of them suggests examples of activities that would continue to seem worthwhile under doomsday or infertility conditions. Although I am not persuaded by all of their examples, I am not sure how much we disagree on the

1. It may be worth noting that Theo Faron says, in James's novel, that what prevents some people from experiencing the "*ennui universel*" is "an egotism so powerful that no external catastrophe can prevail against it" (*The Children of Men*, 9). He does not say that the ennui itself is a manifestation of egotism.

basic issue. On the one hand, I agree that some things would continue to matter to us. On the other hand, Frankfurt and Wolf both agree that some things would cease to matter to us, and that other things might come to matter to us less.[2] And that is really sufficient for my purposes.

At times Wolf appears to attribute to me an extremely strong claim, namely, that the very idea of things mattering would be lost if we believed there were no afterlife. This is evidently how she interprets my comment that "we need humanity to have a future for the very idea that things *matter* to retain a secure place in our conceptual repertoire" (60, Wolf 123). So in addition to proposing examples of activities that would continue to matter to us under doomsday or infertility conditions, she also argues against the strong claim that the very concept of things mattering would be lost. But I meant only what I said. Faced with the prospect of humanity's imminent extinction through universal infertility, many of the things that had previously mattered to us would cease

---

2. Wolf agrees with my observation that many goal-oriented projects would no longer be worth pursuing under doomsday or infertility conditions. However, she says there is nothing more surprising about this than there is about the fact that if the company one works for goes out of business, then one must find a new job. I had argued that the observation has deeper significance, because it reveals the extent to which we ordinarily find goals worth pursuing even if we don't expect them to be achieved until after our deaths. Wolf says that she finds this unsurprising too. Surprising or not, however, it shows that the assumption of an ongoing humanity is presupposed by many of our mundane projects and activities, and it shows how important that assumption is to us. Our choice of projects mightn't have been like this, after all. We might have been creatures who considered it very important to pursue only those goals that we could reasonably expect to realize fully during our own lifetimes. People who left things for future generations to complete might have been considered unsuccessful or imprudent or unlucky. But they are not. We take it for granted that there is value in making progress toward a worthwhile goal whose full realization will be accomplished—if at all—by other people after we are long gone.

to do so, and our confident deployment of the concept of something's *mattering* would be destabilized and rendered insecure. This does not mean that nothing at all would matter to us or that the concept would simply disappear. But it does mean that our ability to apply the concept confidently and unreflectively would be compromised and that the range of activities that seemed to us worthwhile would be drastically diminished. The realm of value, for us, would shrink dramatically, and our lives would be impoverished in consequence. That it is the central point, and it is not clear that either Frankfurt or Wolf rejects it.

Although this point would not be undermined if Frankfurt's and Wolf's proposed examples of activities that would continue to matter to us were compelling, it is nevertheless worth explaining why I am not persuaded by those examples or, at least, not by all of them. Frankfurt believes that listening to music is something that would continue to matter to us under doomsday or infertility conditions, because much of its value to us derives from features that are intrinsic to or inherent in the music itself. To derive value from music, he says, we need make no assumptions about the future of humanity. This line of reasoning is not decisive, however. The rewards we derive from listening to music do not consist simply in a set of brute sensations. They involve more complex states of mind that are sensitive, in ways that are not always obvious, to changes in our background attitudes and beliefs about the world. It is a familiar fact that one's appreciation of music can, on any given occasion, be impaired by anxiety or impatience or preoccupation. P. D. James's intriguing speculation was that many activities whose importance to us appears to derive from what is intrinsic to them might nevertheless lose their appeal for people in the infertility scenario. Hence the significance of the fact that reading books, eating food and drinking wine, appreciating nature, and listening to music were not as enjoyable for Theo Faron as they had previously been. Although many of the rewards of those activities appear independent of our beliefs about what will happen in the future,

James's thought seems to be that our awareness of humanity's disappearance might, in the moment, block our access to those rewards or make it less reliable. And although I'm not sure she's right about that, I'm even less sure that she's wrong.[3]

Frankfurt also believes that intellectual and artistic activities would retain much of their appeal in the doomsday and infertility scenarios. I had suggested, to illustrate my opposing position, that a political philosopher might lose confidence in the value of writing additional articles about the relation between liberty and equality or about the interpretation of Rawls's difference principle. Those examples seem plausible, Frankfurt maintains, only because they involve "overworked issues in political theory" (133) and because the activity of writing articles is unrewarding in itself. But I don't find writing articles unrewarding, and the point I was making is not limited to overworked issues in political theory or any other subject. In fact, I find it hard to think of many issues in political philosophy, overworked or not, that would seem worth pursuing seriously if the disappearance of humanity were imminent. Nor many issues in the philosophy of language or in sociology or in economics or in literary theory. Perhaps there are exceptions, like research in the most theoretical parts of physics and mathematics, though even there I don't think the case is clear-cut, and in any event I feel

---

3. There is one other point worth making here. There is at least a superficial difference between saying that we would lose confidence in, say, the value of literature, and saying that we would lose confidence in the value of our own activity of reading novels. Or again, between losing confidence in the value of music and losing confidence in the value of listening to music. My primary conjectures were about our prospective loss of confidence in the value of our activities in the infertility scenario, but I was not clear or consistent enough about the distinction. And from the assertion that we would lose confidence in the value of listening to music, it may not follow that we would lose confidence in the value of music. There may be room for the thought that, although music might remain valuable, our own activities would no longer be a way of gaining access to or realizing the value of music.

confident that a wide range of intellectual and artistic activities would lose much of their appeal.

As Susan Wolf suggests, this is not because people engaged in such activities need to believe, or normally do believe, that their work will have an impact on the way their chosen field of endeavor develops in the future. It is rather because the perceived point of much scholarly and creative activity depends on seeing oneself as a participant in a collective, temporally extended project. The perceived point or value of my scholarly activities is not independent of the thought that I am part of a larger, temporally extended practice that has endured for thousands of years and that I expect to endure for many more. If I am suddenly confronted with the prospect that it's just me sitting here, writing my measly books and articles, and that I am no longer a participant in a flourishing chain of human conversation and creativity, then I do find myself wondering what the point is. And in a way this is encouraging. It means that, under ordinary rather than doomsday conditions, even very modest academic or creative efforts can have a point or a value that is independent of their individual merits or causal influence, for there is a value to participating in a valuable collaborative project whether or not one has any discernible impact on the character of that project. And surely that is what most writers and artists must believe or hope is true.

Wolf believes that the sorts of activity that would be most likely to retain their appeal under doomsday or infertility conditions are those directed at the care and comfort of others.[4] Not only would people continue to comfort and care for those who were already dying or in immediate need, but they might well extend the same concern to one another in general. I am sure she is right that the impulse to care for others would be a salient feature of many people's reactions to the infertility scenario. But of course this presupposes the truth of my

---

4. In the remainder of this section I will, for simplicity, concentrate on the infertility scenario, but nothing significant turns on this.

main conjecture, namely, that the scenario would be perceived as a catastrophe, and that many of the activities that seem worthwhile under happier conditions would lose much of their appeal. Moreover, one thing that is often comforting under ordinary conditions is precisely the recognition that life goes on and that the world of value continues to thrive. Even if one is severely ill or needy now, one may hope to rejoin that world, and this may make one consolable. And even for the elderly and the dying, the recognition that life will go on can be a source of great solace; contact with young people—grandchildren, perhaps—is often a particular pleasure. None of this would be true in the infertility scenario.

Still, let's suppose, as seems plausible, that lots of people would have the impulse to comfort one another. How would they go about doing this? Wolf writes that "we could create and perform music and plays, we could plant gardens, hold discussion groups, write books and commentaries" (122). I have three worries about this. First, I take it that Wolf's examples are supposed to be representative, rather than exhaustive, of the mutually comforting collective activities in which people would be motivated to participate under infertility conditions. But if I try to expand her list of examples to incorporate a wider range of the group activities that people find enjoyable and rewarding under ordinary conditions, I quickly run up against the following difficulty. In order for people to participate in such activities, there has to be a functioning economy that both supports the activities in question and makes it possible for people to satisfy their general human needs. After all, to take a simple example, if people who did not live on farms were to have time for anything other than foraging, someone would have to be maintaining the food supply in the infertile world. But one of the very points at issue is whether people would still be motivated, under infertility conditions, to play their previous parts in the economic system. The worry, then, is that the very availability of comforting activities like those Wolf mentions presupposes that, contrary to my speculation, most participants in the social division of labor would be willing to engage in business as usual under infertility conditions. Second, even if we set this concern aside, I remain uncertain about the extent to which the activities Wolf has in mind would actually appeal to people under infertility conditions. I find it hard to believe, for example, that very many people would be motivated to write books, plays, and commentaries as a way of comforting one another. Finally, even if there were some shared activities in which people found comfort, the fundamental point I made earlier still holds. Under infertility conditions, the range of activities that seemed to us worthwhile would be drastically diminished, the realm of value would be vastly reduced, and our lives would be severely impoverished in consequence.

Wolf suggests that our involvement in caring activities might enable us to overcome some of the initially destabilizing effects of the infertility scenario and to become reengaged with many more of the activities we had previously valued. So our loss of confidence in the value of those activities might be only temporary. For the reasons I have given, I don't find this very plausible as a general matter. But I agree that some things would continue to matter to people in an infertile world, and that there would be something particularly admirable about people who did not simply give in to despair but who continued to derive as much value as possible from the limited range of available activities that remained capable of supplying it. Frankfurt, after observing that there would doubtless be differences in the ways people reacted to the infertility scenario, draws an analogy between people's reactions under those conditions and the reactions of individuals who discover that they personally have only a short time left to live. Although some of them despair, others determine "to make the most of the time remaining to them, and they devote themselves to enjoying what is valuable and important to them" (136). Many people with whom I have discussed "The Afterlife" have suggested the same analogy. Often they have gone on to point out that some individuals who receive a terminal diagnosis are initially devastated and demoralized, but subsequently bounce back and resolve to make the best use available of the time that remains to them. Extending the analogy in this way affords a different route to Wolf's conclusion that people's loss of confidence under infertility conditions might be only temporary.

I myself don't find the analogy compelling, however. When individuals receive a terminal diagnosis under ordinary conditions, often they resolve to stop wasting time on activities of little value and to devote as much time as possible to valued activities which they may previously have neglected. However, one thing that makes it possible for them to do this, as I have maintained, is precisely their recognition that life goes on and that the world of value continues to thrive. What is painful for them is the realization that they must soon leave that world, which remains as rich as ever. The problem they face is not that the world of value itself is diminished or eroding. But, if I am right, that is exactly how things would seem to people in the infertility scenario. The problem with which they would be confronted is not the problem of having an undiminished supply of worthwhile activities but only a limited time in which to engage in them. Instead, their problem would be that there were so few activities that seemed worth engaging in at all. The world of value itself would be slipping away like a fistful of sand.

The Alvy Singer Problem

Most of us believe that the human race will die out someday, but this does not undermine our confidence in the value of the activities in which we are now engaged. The afterlife conjecture holds, however, that if we thought that humanity's extinction were imminent, this *would* cause us to lose confidence in the value of many of those same activities. What are we to make of the discrepancy between these two reactions? We can call this the Alvy Singer problem.

One response to the problem is to assert that there is rational pressure to react the same way in the two cases, and that the way we should react in both cases is by losing confidence in the value of our activities. We might think of this as the Alvy Singer solution. A different response is to agree that there is rational pressure to react the same way in the two cases, but to assert that the way we should react in both cases is by retaining confidence in the value of our activities. This is the solution that Wolf favors.

A third response is to deny that there really is rational pressure to react the same way in the two cases. According to this response, there may be good reasons for us to react differently to the prospect of humanity's disappearance in the distant future than we do to the prospect of its imminent disappearance. Perhaps, for example, the eventual disappearance of humanity need not be threatening so long as it does not occur before human beings have had enough time to achieve all of their most valuable aims and to realize all of their most valuable ideals. Or perhaps, if the prospect of humanity's disappearance is very remote, there may still be time for our more knowledgeable and perhaps more intelligent descendants to find ways of avoiding it. And so on.

In Lecture 2, I mentioned a fourth response. This response holds that our reaction (or lack of reaction) to the prospect of humanity's extinction in the distant future is an unreliable guide to our evaluative beliefs. It is unreliable because, in order to contemplate that prospect, we must take up a temporal perspective whose vast scale is sufficiently unfamiliar that we have no basis in our experience for making confident judgments from that perspective. So it is misguided to compare our reactions in the two cases.

Despite having suggested this last response, I am not sure that it is correct, and I do not claim to have a solution to the Alvy Singer problem. Whereas Wolf finds the second response compelling, I find it no more plausible than any of the others. What I do know is that I find the afterlife conjecture convincing as an empirical prediction about how people would react. As a normative matter, moreover,

I do not think people would be making a general or systematic mistake if they were to react as the afterlife conjecture predicts that they would. This is, of course, compatible with allowing that a particular person might make a mistake in thinking, with respect to some activity, that it either was or was not worth pursuing under doomsday or infertility conditions. And it is compatible with my earlier observation that there would be something especially admirable about people who did not simply give in to despair but instead tried to derive as much value as possible from the limited range of activities that remained worth pursuing.

Now and Then

Frankfurt conjectures that we might also lose confidence in the value of many of our activities if we came to believe not that there would be no people in the future, but rather that we had no contemporaries, that we were alone in the world at present. I agree. Indeed, I see even less chance than he does that one might lead a worthwhile life if one lacked contemporaries. However, this doesn't mean that our confidence does not also depend on our belief in the existence of the afterlife. In the infertility scenario, people have contemporaries, but—as I believe, and as Frankfurt seems to agree at least in part—they would nevertheless lose confidence in the value of many of their activities. The two conjectures—one about the present and the other about the future—are not mutually exclusive, they are complementary. As he says, they are both examples or symptoms of the limits of our individualism. But he also suggests that confidence in the existence of the afterlife is not our basic or fundamental concern. What we most basically need, if we are to lead value-laden lives, is confidence in the existence of other people who are somehow aware of us, whether those people exist now or in the future. However, in the infertility scenario, people are aware of one another, so the absence of such awareness cannot explain why they would lose confidence in the value of their activities. And although, as I emphasized in Lecture 1, it is important to many people that they be remembered for awhile after they are gone, this also cannot explain the loss of confidence occasioned by the prospect of humanity's imminent extinction. People would suffer the same loss of confidence even if they had already been convinced, before learning of the impending disaster, that nobody in the next generation would remember them personally anyway.

Conservatism and Humanity

Seana Shiffrin's sensitive and insightful comments raise a number of fascinating issues. The first of these has to do with what I called the *conservative dimension* of our attitudes toward the things that we value. Shiffrin makes it clear that this dimension of our attitudes is complex. My own treatment of it was cursory, and an adequate treatment would require much more refinement. For one thing, Shiffrin points out that there are cases in which we don't want the particular things that we value to be preserved indefinitely. As examples she mentions particular musical performances, conversations, and meals. With some of these things, she suggests, it seems plausible to say that their value derives from the value of the types they instantiate, and that although we want the type to continue to be instantiated, we do not want any instance of the type to continue indefinitely.

It is worth noting, though, that Shiffrin's clearest examples of particular things that we value but do not want preserved are all *events*, like meals or performances. And in these cases, as she observes, the point may be less that we resist preservation of the valuable item than that the valuable item cannot be preserved as such by being prolonged. Temporal extension does not preserve it as a valuable item but rather transforms it into something less valuable. Furthermore, there are other cases in which we do want the particular items that we value to be preserved indefinitely. This seems true, for example, of our attitudes toward particular objects like great paintings or features of the natural environment. It also seems true of our attitudes toward friendships and other close personal relationships. Insofar as we value our friendships, we normally want to preserve or sustain them. In this respect, they are more like paintings and less like meals or conversations. Then there is the case of personal projects. On the one hand, there are some projects that I value, but which I do not want to persist indefinitely. I may value my project of building a house, but I do not want it to last forever. On the other hand, there are more open-ended projects, like maintaining a garden or preserving a redwood forest. In some cases, whether we want to sustain a personal project indefinitely may depend on how the project is described. A laboratory scientist may not want a particular experiment to take forever, but she may well want to continue carrying out her research program indefinitely and to contribute to the growth of scientific knowledge for as long as she can.

So our conservatism about value is complex, and care is required in specifying the objects and the character of our conservative attitudes. In addition, as Shiffrin notes, our conservatism coexists uneasily with other attitudes that we have, and especially with our strong interest in expressing our creativity by developing new practices and forms of activity. In fact, even our conservatism cannot adequately be characterized in exclusively static terms. To preserve a valuable institution in changing circumstances may require the institution itself to change.[5] Conservatism of the relevant sort is not always a matter of preserving the status quo. In addition, though, conservatism is not

5. This is a point I have developed at greater length elsewhere. See "Conceptions of Cosmopolitanism," *Utilitas* 11 (1999): 255–76, reprinted in *Boundaries and Allegiances* (New York: Oxford University Press, 2001), 111–30; and "Immigration and the Significance of Culture," *Philosophy & Public Affairs* 35 (2007): 93–125, reprinted in *Equality and Tradition*, 256–86.

always a viable stance all things considered, as Shiffrin emphasizes. Even valuable practices and traditions must sometimes give way in order to make room for new ones, given the limited social space available for the realization of diverse values and the impossibility of making room in our lives for all valuable things at once. Conservative though we may be in some respects, she suggests, we can contemplate with acceptance, if not with relish, the fading away of valued practices to make way for new ones, provided that the older practices are superseded for good reasons. An adequate characterization of our conservatism must include a qualification to this effect.

These reflections lead Shiffrin to suspect that even if our conservative attitudes are given a suitably nuanced characterization, they cannot fully explain the strength of our reactions to the infertility scenario. It cannot be the bare prospect that all of our valuable practices will come to an end that is so disturbing, because that prospect would not be intolerable if those practices were superseded by other practices that had been developed for good reasons and which expressed or instantiated genuine values of some kind. What is so distressing about the infertility scenario, she speculates, is that our practices would all come to an end *"for no adequate justificatory reason"* (153). Or, to put it more affirmatively, what our reactions to the infertility scenario reveal is the importance we attach to the persistence, not of the practices we now value, but of the abstract activity of valuing itself.

I find Shiffrin's insightful suggestions generally sympathetic, but there is one point that I need to clarify. I do not believe that our conservatism about the particular things that we value provides the primary explanation of our predicted reactions to the infertility scenario. So I don't attach as much weight to the conservatism thesis as she thinks that I do. Although I do believe that our reactions reveal the conservative dimension of our valuing attitudes, as well as their nonexperiential and nonconsequentialist dimensions, my main point was that those reactions also bring out something deeper, namely, the importance that we attach to the survival of humanity itself.

In other words, my conjecture was that if we were actually confronted with the infertility scenario, our reactions would not be limited to dismay at the prospect that the particular practices we valued were going to die out. They would also include a loss of confidence in the value of continuing to engage in those practices even before they had died out. And I argued that our predicted loss of confidence reveals that what matters to us here and now implicitly depends on our assumption that humanity will survive.

We can, of course, ask which features of humanity are responsible for the loss of evaluative confidence that would be occasioned by the prospect of its imminent disappearance. This is to ask, in effect, which features of humanity itself we value. I am sure that Shiffrin is right to suggest, in a Kantian spirit, that the general capacity of human beings to engage in valuing activity, and their even more general capacity to respond to reasons, must have a prominent place in any adequate answer to this question. However, I am not convinced that these capacities provide the complete answer. Although I don't have firm views about this, my feeling is that we are more attached to the specifically human than Shiffrin is inclined to suppose. That may partly be because I think history counts for more than she does, and partly because I think biology counts for more. If human beings were to die out and be superseded by a different kind of rational, valuing creature, and if those posthuman creatures remembered us with appreciation but had their own values, then I agree that might be better than nothing: better than an alternative in which valuing and reason-based thought and practice disappeared from the world altogether. But I still think it would be a major loss. We do not regard ourselves as being, so to speak, just one format in which rational agency and valuing attitudes may be instantiated, such that we could be superseded by another format without significant loss, in something like the way LPs were superseded by compact discs (although even in that case there was loss).

Consider, for example, the role played by our specifically human embodiment in determining the content of many of our values and valued activities and forms of expression. This is especially clear with respect to the arts—including, obviously, painting, sculpture, dance and music and also, only slightly less obviously, literature, theater, and poetry. But it is true of many other values and valued activities as well: think, for instance, of the values we attach to sex, sports, play, child rearing, and the pleasures of the table. Even many of our moral values are shaped by our biological and psychological natures: by our sense of a normal life span, of the normal stages of life, of our specific capacities and vulnerabilities, of our susceptibility to pleasure and pain, of our need for material resources, and so on. I think that very few of our values could simply be detached from our biological natures, and many of them only make sense in particular historical and social contexts. So I am somewhat more attached to the human than Shiffrin is, and my own suspicion is that the disappearance of specifically human life would have a more profound impact than she is inclined to believe. Suppose, for example, that rational creatures with different histories and radically different material constitutions were to take our place—creatures who arrived from outer space, say, made up of elements not found on earth and taking a physical form that struck us as hideous. If those creatures recognized reasons, knew about us and our history, appreciated our value, and had genuine values but ones very different from our own—values suited to their natures and histories rather than ours—then, as I said, I suppose that might be better than nothing. But I think that I, unlike Shiffrin, would still find the end of human life profoundly depressing.

This means that I am drawn to an intermediate position. I agree with Shiffrin that our dismay at the infertility scenario does not derive solely from the prospect that the specific projects and practices that we now value will disappear. But neither do I think it derives solely from the prospect that valuing and reason-based practices in general will disappear. On the one hand, our confidence in the value of our existing activities is not jeopardized by our recognition that the values of future humans are bound to differ in some important respects from our own. But, on the other hand, our confidence would not be secured, in the face of the infertility scenario, simply by the knowledge that nonhuman creatures would succeed us and that they would engage in rational, valuing practices of some kind. Of course, matters might be different, in the first case, if we thought that our human successors and their values would be thoroughly and irredeemably depraved, and matters might be different, in the second case, if we thought that our nonhuman successors and their values would be very similar to us and our values. But this doesn't change the basic point.

I do think Shiffrin is correct to observe that there is an analogue on the collective level of the asymmetry Lucretius noted on the individual level between our attitudes toward prenatal and post-mortem nonexistence. It is a very good point. Our prior collective nonexistence is not remotely as distressing as is the prospect that there will be no collective afterlife. This has implications for how the importance of human history should be understood. I said in Lecture 2 that our valuing attitudes implicitly depend on the assumption that human life "is an ongoing phenomenon with a history that transcends the history of any individual" (59). I was understanding "human history" broadly, as incorporating both the human past and the human future. But this masks an important difference between the past and the future. As Shiffrin says, the Lucretian asymmetry, as it applies to humanity as a whole, manifests itself in the following difference: the human past matters if there has been a human past, whereas the human future matters whether there will be one or not. Of course, since we know that there has been a human past, it follows that both matter.

The Fear of Death and the Value of Life

In his characteristically incisive comments, Niko Kolodny expresses reservations about a number of the views I defend in Lecture 3. He begins by attributing to me two main theses:

A. We have reason to fear death, independently of its "depriving" us of the goods of future life, because it "extinguishes" us: brings it about that we no longer exist.

B. If we never died, we would not live (stronger conclusion) a life at all, or (weaker conclusion) a value-laden life.

And he says that I draw (or seem to draw) two conclusions from B:

C. Never dying but still living a life, or never dying but still living a value-laden life, is conceptually incoherent.

D. Never dying would be a disaster for us, since it would deprive us of a life, or a value-laden life.

Kolodny develops three main lines of thought. First, he suggests some "striking implications" of A. Second, he raises some questions about the interpretation and implications of C and D. Third, he offers some objections to B, and suggests a weaker thesis that may be more defensible. I will consider these lines of thought in turn.

1. Kolodny argues that A (in combination with some additional premises that he finds independently plausible) implies three conclusions that he labels H, J, and K. Taken together, these conclusions amount to the claim that "insofar as it is not fear of the deprivation of the goods of further life, our fear of death may be, unlike any other fear, a fear of something that we have no reason to avoid, something that is in no way bad for us, and something whose analogue in the past gives us not the slightest disquiet to contemplate" (164). We can label this claim Q. Kolodny believes that since A implies Q, and since I endorse A, I am committed to Q. As I have said, Kolodny regards Q as a striking claim. Yet he also observes that even if A implies Q, that need not refute A. Q may, in the end, be true, and its truth may testify only to the "singularity" of our fear of death.

I am of two minds about how to respond to this line of thought. On the one hand, as Kolodny notes, one of the things I was trying to do in Lecture 3 was precisely to emphasize the "strange and sui generis" (85) character of the fear of death. Given the kind of thing death is, it is not surprising that the fear of death should, in various ways, be unlike any other fear. Death amounts to personal extinction, as Kolodny says, and there is nothing quite like extinction. So it would hardly be surprising if the fear of extinction were unlike any other fear. Q may simply reflect that fact.

On the other hand, I am not sure that I am really committed to Q. I have two reasons for doubting this. First, Kolodny's primary argument from A to H and J, which are two of the three components of Q, relies on the independent premise:

F. There is no egoistic reason to avoid extinction as such.

Kolodny accepts F because he thinks that for a sufficiently unfortunate person, someone for whom the evils of future life outweigh the goods, the bare fact that death involves extinction provides *no* egoistic reason to avoid death. The fact that the prospective evils of continued life outweigh the goods simply settles the deliberative question. Indeed, he thinks that to suppose otherwise is to commit something like a category mistake. But I don't find this obvious. To me it seems that, even in the circumstances described, someone might find the fact that death involved personal extinction to be a consideration in favor of avoiding it, albeit a consideration that might well be outweighed if the balance of prospective evils over prospective goods were sufficiently great. I don't think that such a person would be unreasonable or guilty of a category mistake.

One possible rejoinder to this is to suggest that, in taking the prospect of extinction to provide a reason for avoiding death, I am smuggling into the idea of extinction considerations that really belong under the heading of deprivation of future goods. In other words, I am tacitly relying on the fact that extinction will deprive me of things like future consciousness and self-consciousness. But to the extent that being deprived of those things counts as a reason to avoid death, it must be because they count as future goods.

And in Kolodny's example, these and other future goods have, by hypothesis, already been taken into account and judged insufficient to outweigh future evils, so it would be a kind of double-counting to consider them again. Now I am uncertain about the claim that, if the deprivation of future consciousness and self-consciousness counts as a reason to avoid death, it must be because those things count as future goods. It seems to me at least as plausible to think that the reverse is true. If the deprivation of future consciousness and self-consciousness counts as the deprivation of future goods, it is because they are things one has reason to avoid. Nevertheless, the reply points to a real lack of clarity in the distinction between what falls under the heading of extinction and what falls under the heading of future deprivation. And that leads to my second reason for doubting whether I am really committed to Q.

Put simply, the reason is that I'm not sure that I accept A, despite the fact that Kolodny interprets it as one of my two main theses. To begin with, the first part of A—the phrase "we have reason to fear death"—needs to be handled with care. Some people fear death and some don't. Among those who do, not all of them fear the same thing. So "the fear of death" may not be a unified phenomenon. What some people fear, for example, may be that the process of dying will be painful or undignified. Other people may instead fear, albeit in a confused way, that the experience of being dead will be unpleasant. Others may be afraid because they are unsure what will happen to them when they die. And still others may fear that they will miss out on future events that they long to witness or participate in. But there is also another kind of fear to which many (though not all) people are subject: a fear—even a kind of terror or panic—induced by the thought that I myself will simply stop being. My question was whether this kind of fear can be reasonable for people who are subject to it. Although I defended an affirmative answer to this question, I did not mean to suggest that those who are not subject to such fear are unreasonable. Nor did I mean to suggest that this kind of fear is reasonable under all conditions. As my example of the Epicurean torturer was meant to indicate, I think that there are conditions in which it is reasonable to welcome and even long for death.

A goes on to assert that our reason to fear death is independent of the fact that death deprives us of future goods. This is a slightly stronger claim than any I want to endorse. As I observed, the deprivation theory, as normally understood, seeks to explain why death is bad for the person who dies. It is bad because it deprives the person of future goods. The theory is not ordinarily presented as an account of why the fear of death is reasonable. If it were so interpreted, it would presumably hold that it is reasonable to fear death because death deprives one of future goods. We could call this the deprivation theory, part II, or simply DT II. My thought was that, although some people do fear death because it will deprive them of future goods, the kind of fear that I was considering does not seem naturally described in those terms. So DT II does not seem fully satisfying on its face.

This may be, in part, because of some of the connotations of the term "deprivation." When we say that a person has been deprived of something, this may in some contexts suggest that the person was entitled to that thing, or that she had an epistemically reasonable expectation of getting it. But, insofar as we fear death, that is not in general because we think we are entitled to avoid it or because we have an epistemically reasonable belief that we will avoid it. So talk of deprivation may be misleading here. In addition, such talk fails to distinguish between goods that we now possess, but will cease to possess when we die, and goods that we do not now possess, but would come to possess if we lived longer. The kind of fear I am interested in is focused more on the former than the latter; it is a response to the recognition that I myself will simply stop being, rather than to the prospect of forgoing things I would attain for the first time if I lived longer. So I find it more natural to say that the object of this sort of fear is the prospect that I myself—the thinker of my thoughts, the perceiver of what I perceive—will simply cease to exist, that my mental and physical life will end, that I will be extinguished. I lack the emotional and conceptual resources fully to assimilate this idea, and that induces terror.

Now perhaps, in the end, this kind of fear can, despite my reservations, be brought under the umbrella of DT II. That will depend on whether DT II can be interpreted in such a way as to do justice to the character of such fear and to eliminate the potentially misleading associations imported by the term "deprivation." Perhaps, for example, DT II should be reformulated in such a way as to avoid the word "deprivation" altogether. Perhaps it should be interpreted as asserting that I have reason to fear death because death means that, in the future, I will not have certain goods (including the goods of consciousness and self-consciousness) that (a) I now have, and (b) I would continue to have if I did not die. And perhaps there is no difference between this kind of fear and the fear of my own extinction. Perhaps, in other words, there is no difference between being afraid of my own extinction or cessation, on the one hand, and being afraid of my nonpossession in the future of certain things (like consciousness and self-consciousness) that I now possess. So insofar as I am terrified at the prospect of my extinction or cessation, perhaps that is, after all, no different from being terrified at the prospect that I will not possess certain goods in the future. I am neutral about the truth of these claims. If defenders of the deprivation theory can establish their truth, then I have no stake in insisting, as A does, that our reasons to fear death are independent of considerations about future goods. My only concern is to make sure that the objects of our fear have been properly identified. I want to be sure that we have accurately characterized the kind of fear whose reasonableness is at stake.

2. In Lecture 3 I wrote: "When we are tempted, as many of us are at times, to wish that our lives could go on forever, often what we are wishing is that some version of the lives we are now leading could continue without end: an improved version, perhaps, but a recognizable version nonetheless. If what I have been saying is even

roughly correct, however, the wish is confused" (100). It is confused because eternal existence would undermine the conditions that make the lives we are now leading possible. Kolodny asks: what follows from this? I suppose it does follow, to answer his next question, that the wish is in one way unreasonable. But, as he suggests, it is not unreasonable to regret the fact that eternal existence would undermine the conditions that make the lives we are now leading possible. It is not unreasonable to regret that it is conceptually impossible to have it both ways. Kolodny goes on to ask: what should we make of the fact that the desire for a worthwhile eternal life and the desire never to die are so widespread if, by hypothesis, a worthwhile eternal life is conceptually impossible and never dying would be a disaster for us? What I make of it is this: the fact that these desires are so intense and widespread is a symptom of how much we love being alive. It is not at all surprising that our love of being alive should lead us to form desires that are in some ways unreasonable or confused. Kolodny suggests that if we interpret people as desiring not infinite time but simply more time than they have, then we can attribute to them a reasonable structure of desire. I agree that this alternative structure of desire is reasonable. But since I am less uncomfortable than he is with the idea of ascribing to people the desire for an eternal life, even if that desire is unreasonable, I feel less pressure than he perhaps thinks I should to insist that they do not have the desire after all.[6]

3. Kolodny is not persuaded by the arguments for B. One argument asserts that a life (or a value-laden life) requires a progression through stages. Kolodny replies that an infinite life could involve a progression through stages. A second argument asserts that a life (or a value-laden life) requires the possibility of loss, illness, injury,

---

6. However, my willingness to assert that the desire is in some ways unreasonable means that I need to amend what I said in the final paragraph of Lecture 3, where I purported to identify the *only* point at which our attitudes toward death are unreasonable.

harm, risk, and danger, and that these concepts draw much of their content from the possibility of death. Kolodny replies that much of their content is nevertheless independent of the possibility of death. A third argument asserts that temporal scarcity is a necessary condition for valuing. Kolodny replies that even an eternal life would be subject to some forms of temporal scarcity.

However, my first argument was not merely that our lives involve a progression through stages, but that "we understand a human life as having stages, beginning with birth and ending with death," and that this understanding exerts a pervasive influence on the content of our values. An infinite life could not have a trajectory of this kind.

My second argument, meanwhile, does not deny that the concepts in question would retain any of their content if we lived forever, but it does maintain that it is a real question how much. Kolodny lists various forms of harm or misfortune that he believes would persist under conditions of immortality. Perhaps he is right about some of them, but my point was that this is less clear than it may initially seem. Our experiences of dishonor, loss of reputation, and humiliation, to take three of his examples, reflect our understanding of what it means to live a finite life well. These experiences are partly constituted by attitudes of self-assessment, and they are typically occasioned by interactions with others and by the attitudes we take those others to have toward us. As such, they depend heavily on our sense of ourselves, on the ideals we aspire to realize, and on the place we wish to occupy in our social world. Yet the conditions of life for eternal beings would be so remote from ours that it is difficult to arrive at even the haziest understanding of what sense of self such beings might have, of what their social world might be like, or of the ways in which their attitudes toward themselves might depend on the attitudes of others. For this reason, it seems to me a mistake to proceed by first treating the content of concepts like dishonor, reputation, and humiliation as fixed by our current understanding, and then suspending in imagination the assumption of finitude and supposing the concepts to apply unchanged within an eternal life. Although their content can be specified without any explicit reference to our mortality, these concepts nevertheless acquire the content they do in the context of the lives of mortals, and we cannot be sure whether eternal beings would develop them at all or, if so, what role they would play in the attitudes and deliberations of such creatures. More generally, we cannot simply assume that the values that figure so centrally in our actual lives would play a comparable role—or any role—in an eternal life.

Finally, the observation that some forms of temporal scarcity would persist in an eternal life strikes me as true but of uncertain significance. Consider first an analogy. Hume thought that a moderate scarcity of material resources was among the circumstances of justice. Given unlimited resources, the virtue of justice would lose its point. Someone might reply that even given unlimited resources, some forms of scarcity would persist. Even in a world where there were unlimited grapefruits within easy reach of every single person, for example, the opportunity to consume any particular grapefruit would still be scarce. Does this show that the moderate scarcity Hume had in mind is not really among the circumstances of justice? No. Humean moderate scarcity may still be the kind of scarcity on which justice depends for its point. Similarly, my claim is not that there would be nothing at all that could be called "temporal scarcity" in a life without end, but rather that the finiteness of our actual lives represents a particularly significant and consequential form of temporal scarcity. It is this kind of scarcity, I conjecture, that helps to explain how the attitude of valuing comes to play such an important role in human life. Absent this kind of scarcity, it is at best unclear to what extent we would be guided by ideas of value at all. The bare fact that, in an eternal life, there would still be other things that could be considered forms of temporal scarcity settles nothing by itself.

However, Kolodny's point was not merely that there would be some forms of temporal scarcity in an eternal life, but that some *valuable* items would be subject to this form of scarcity. In the comparison case mentioned earlier, no particular grapefruit would have any special value as compared with other grapefruits. By contrast, Kolodny suggests, even an eternal life might be subject to temporal scarcity with respect to positional goods such as particular marriage partners or opportunities to invent particular things or to make particular discoveries. Similarly, one might run the risk of being separated forever from someone one loved.

One problem in thinking about such examples is that it is difficult to be sure one is not smuggling into one's reflections the very conclusions one is trying to establish. That is because the recognition of our mortality exerts such a deep and pervasive influence on our thinking that when trying to imagine what the lives of eternal beings would be like, it is difficult to be sure that one has eliminated all traces of that influence. So, for instance, it is far from clear to me that it would ever occur to eternal beings to construct the distinctive form of personal partnership that we call a marriage, or what biological, emotional, or practical imperatives might lead them to do this. Indeed, it is difficult even to be sure that such beings would be subject to love and the other forms of value-laden attachment to others with which we are familiar. To a degree I find difficult to estimate, these forms of selective attachment are themselves shaped by the familiar facts of temporal scarcity: by the recognition that, in the time available to us, we can only interact and spend time with a tiny handful of people.

More generally, I find it hard to form any very definite conception of what the practical reasoning of eternal beings would be like or of what sorts of things would count for them as reasons for action. Perhaps we can imagine that, in some versions of eternity, conditions might obtain (such as the prospect of eternal separation from particular people) that mimicked the effects of death and so restored something like the kind of temporal scarcity I believe to be important. Of course, the greater the number of such conditions that we insist on, the less likely it is that the resulting form of eternal existence will answer to the hopes and wishes that have led people to long for immortality. Still, I concede that some of the forms of temporal scarcity to which eternal beings were subject might put a degree of pressure on them to develop value concepts and apply them to features of their world. Even so, I am convinced that the finiteness of our lives exerts an extremely powerful influence on our actual development and deployment of value concepts. At the very least, we have no good reason to think that beings who were not subject to this particular form of temporal scarcity would have values anything like ours.

In light of his objections to B, Kolodny suggests two weaker theses that might be easier to defend and might serve my purposes just as well. The first is

M. If we never died, we would not live a *human* life, or a life laden with *human* values, because no life that went on forever would be a *human* life, or a *human* value-laden life.

Even better, he thinks, would be

N. The lives that we are now in the midst of leading could not continue to be laden with the *values that they actually are* were we never to die, because *those* values presuppose our death.

Now, of course, B was not my formulation in the first place. It represents Kolodny's understanding of what I was claiming. That understanding is not unreasonable, although, as he notes in a footnote, my frequent use of the term "human" suggests something closer to M. But Kolodny worries that M sounds too much like something I wanted to avoid. It sounds too much like a "trivial truth resting on a stipulative definition" (100) of *human*. Hence his preference for N. I agree with him that the differences among these propositions may not make much practical or emotional difference. Still, I would like my position to be defensible and it is important to state it clearly. What I want to say, then, is the following. If we never died, then we would not live lives structured by the kinds of values that now structure our own lives or by the kinds of values that have structured the lives of other human beings now and in the past. Moreover, it is at best unclear to what extent we would lead value-structured lives at all. What *is* clear, in any case, is that we would not live anything resembling what we now consider to be "a life." So the fantasy that the lives we are now leading might continue forever is inherently confused and in principle unsatisfiable.

Index